I0496009

OPTIONS TRADING

A BEGINNER'S SECRET TO SUCCESS ON
THE OPTIONS TRADING. LEARN THE
ADVANCED TECHNIQUE FOR
CONTROLLING THE STOCK MARKET
AND ESTABLISH A SOLID SOURCE OF
INCOME

Andrew Matthew Warren

1

Options Trading

© **Copyright 2020 - All rights reserved.**

The content contained within this book may not be reproduced, duplicated or transmitted without direct written permission from the author or the publisher.

Under no circumstances will any blame or legal responsibility be held against the publisher, or author, for any damages, reparation, or monetary loss due to the information contained within this book. Either directly or indirectly.

Legal Notice: This book is copyright protected. This book is only for personal use. You cannot amend, distribute, sell, use, quote or paraphrase any part, or the content within this book, without the consent of the author or publisher.

Disclaimer Notice: Please note the information contained within this document is for educational and entertainment purposes only. All effort has been executed to present accurate, up to date, and reliable, complete information. No warranties of any kind are declared or implied. Readers acknowledge that the author is not engaging in the rendering of legal, financial, medical or professional advice. The content within this book has been derived from various sources. Please consult a licensed professional before attempting any techniques outlined in this book.

By reading this document, the reader agrees that under no circumstances is the author responsible for any losses, direct or indirect, which are incurred as a result of the use of information contained within this document, including, but not limited to, — errors, omissions, or inaccuracies.

TABLE OF CONTENTS

INTRODUCTION 4

CHAPTER 1.   MINDSET 6

CHAPTER 2.   HOW OPTIONS PRICES ARE DETERMINED....................14

CHAPTER 3.   HOW TO GET STARTED IN OPTIONS TRADING 21

CHAPTER 4.   REASONS WHY OPTIONS TRADING IS BETTER THAN STOCK

TRADING 30

CHAPTER 5.   BASICS OPTIONS STRATEGIES GOING LONG 33

CHAPTER 6.   OPTION RISK AND REWARD 40

CHAPTER 7.   UNDERSTANDING OPTIONS RISKS 46

CHAPTER 8.   DEVELOPMENT OF THE OPTION 50

CHAPTER 9.   CONCEPTS BEHIND OPTIONS................................59

CHAPTER 10.   GOOD RESOURCES AND THEIR IMPORTANCE IN OPTION

TRADING   62

CHAPTER 11.   ANALYZING MOOD SWING IN THE MARKET 66

CHAPTER 12.   SECTOR ANALYSIS: TECHNICAL AND FUNDAMENTAL 74

CHAPTER 13.   ROLLING OUT OPTIONS 84

CHAPTER 14.   DESIGNING A TRADING PLAN 89

CHAPTER 15.   ADVANCED STRATEGIES 96

CHAPTER 16.   KEY TO A SUCCESSFUL OPTIONS TRADING 107

CHAPTER 17.   TOP TRADER MISTAKES TO AVOID IN OPTIONS TRADING.....114

CONCLUSION 123

Introduction

The options market is a great choice for those who do not mind losing a little potential reward in exchange for extra protection against losses. That does not mean that there isn't the possibility for major returns, you just need to know where to look. With practice, these types of returns will become more and more obvious until you reach the point where you will not believe you did not see them the entire time. If you feel like you are on your way to this point and that you just need a little extra help making it over the top then you have come to the right place, Options Trading: Advanced Options Trading Tips, Tricks & Trends is here to provide you with the last details you need to become a true expert in options trader.

Why trade options instead of the stock itself? As we'll learn later in this book, options can be used in a variety of ways to take advantage and profit from the inherent rise and fall of the markets. Options offer an array of solid trading strategies utilizing put and call options in abundant trade scenarios.

I'll mention one strategy to show you how options can be used with your current stock trading, but we'll go into greater details. Options can be used to ensure your current holdings of stocks from a decline or increase, depending on if you are long or short. To explain the concept, you probably have insurance on your car or house against damage and loss of those assets. Options give the same type of safety net for stocks and investments.

Options offer protection against a market price decline of the underlying stock or an increase in the market price of the underlying stock, depending on if you are holding it long (speculating an increase) or short (speculating a decrease).

Options can facilitate a lower-priced stock purchase by exercising an in-the-money call option or sell a stock at a higher price by exercising an in-the-money put option. They can also provide an opportunity to create added income against a short or long stock position you are already holding.

Financial derivatives have been around for at least 200 hundred years since the Japanese introduced the first secondary market for derivatives related to commodities. Nevertheless, they made their debut in the U.S. after the Chicago Board of Trade was founded, in 1848, to organize commodities trading activities. These markets introduced futures and opened the doors for many new financial instruments including options. We will explain the basics of how options work and how they are usually employed in today's modern financial markets.

An option is a contract between two parties giving the taker (buyer) the right, but not the obligation, to buy or sell a security at a predetermined price on or before a predetermined date. To acquire this right, the taker pays a premium to the writer (seller) of the contract.

Chapter 1 Mindset

Options trading is a great way to earn a profit, but many people find it difficult and complicated. Options trading is suitable for beginners as well as experts. This contains detailed information regarding options trading and how you can perform it efficiently.

You need to get rid of the limiting belief that what you are currently is all you can be. You need to have a mindset that promotes growth. Your mindset is your frame of mind. It is the things that you believe, your thoughts and your opinions. Your education thus far, your upbringing, your religion and many other things shape your mindset. Thus, your mindset determines how you perceived the outside world, yourself and what you can achieve.

Your attitude is a manifestation of your mindset and it shows whether your mindset is limiting you or helping your grow. A growth mindset is one that encourages making in extra time and effort to grow intelligence and experience to make a better standard of living. On the other, a fixed mindset is one where it is believed that all our qualities are fixed and born talent is the only fact determining success. This type of mindset limits a person's capacity for learning while a growth mindset is one where there is no limit to potential or success.

What do we understand by the expression "Contributing Mindset?" Essentially, it is about the mental and intellectual nature of the financial expert. Remember, contributing is as a lot of a mental intermingling as it is a series of skill and data. To be sure, even with the best of abilities and all-around data, you are most likely not going to win as a fiscal expert if you don't have the right contributing viewpoint. The right risk perspective, essentially, is a blend of six key characteristics. Over time, it is the right contributing attitude that will have the greatest impact upon developing the skills of a good financial expert and a consistently productive auditor.

1. Mental balance is the key

What do we fathom by mental prudence? It is the ability to think indisputably despite when markets are unusual, and the financial expert is under tremendous weight. Usually, this is when most financial expert will as a rule sway and accept veritable contributing failures. Believe it or not, mental aptitude is about the calm that you can keep up despite when the market appears to go against you. There are extremely two perspectives to mental balance. Stock exchanges are driven by fear and insatiability. Ordinarily, financial experts will when all is said in done get energetic at the most elevated purpose of the market and terrible at the base of the market. Smart contributing is connected to doing the cautious reverse. For example, if you had kept up your balance at the market lows of 2003 and 2009, by then you would have ended up with surprising assumptions at remarkable costs.

2. Not just peace of mind; you also require balance

How definitely is balance unique in connection to peace of mind? What makes a difference is extremely unnoticeable, however, notwithstanding all that it exists. For example, self-restraint is connected to being terrible or greedy in the business sectors at the opportune times. If you get this mix wrong, you could end up with mishaps. Parity is about the point of view wherein you take decisions. A segment of the basic principles are: avoid choosing huge endeavor decisions when you are in a state of ire or dissatisfaction; similarly, avoid investment decisions when you are in a state of uneasiness or doubt; above all, keep away from taking authentic venture decisions in a state of vitality, since you are well while in transit to overextend yourself.

3. Do whatever it takes not to seek after returns, seek after the right framework.

If you are more focused on the results rather than the technique, if you are more worried over the closures than about the strategies, by then you have an attitude problem with respect to contributing. Remember, contributing is substantially more of getting the framework right. How you recognize stocks, how you screen stocks, what are the non-cash related parameters you consider, how might you impact on the channel and the boundaries of security, how might you incorporate a motivation by aligning your passage and leave levels; all these are a bit of your methodology or system. Your consideration should be on fulfilling this methodology and the results will thusly come after.

4. Act generally determined and be a self-motivated student

The stock exchange is a remarkable teacher yet to really take in the fundamental activities from the market, you should be an excited observer and a self-motivated student. The best way to deal with gain from the market is to listen energetically to what the market is trying to tell you. Endeavor to record the learnings from the market consistently and it can transform into your Bible for exchanging. The embodiment of the issue is that your viewpoint should be that of a self-student. The market isn't the place you will be demonstrated the nuances. It is a monstrous gathering of data from which you can liberally draw upon.

5. Be humble to recognize challenges and your mistakes

If you don't practice calmness in your practices, then contributing isn't for you. The best of financial experts gets their assumptions wrong. Attempt to be humble enough to concede that you weren't right and make appropriate helpful change (s). If pride drives you to either average the position or outflank the market, by then you will have a certifiable attitude problem when you are contributing. Recognize that the market has a lot to demonstrate to you and recognize your mistakes. That is the route into the right contributing attitude.

6. An ounce of movement justifies a pound of orchestrating

You can make the best of plans within the planning stage before trading. There are a couple of things about the stock exchanges that you can adjust just once you start exchanging with real money. Amusement can simply take you so far! Grasp a frame of mind that is action planned rather than delighting a great deal in craftiness.

You need to develop a growth mindset for you to move from your current financial position to one where you are financially free. The characteristics of someone who has a growth mindset include:

- Believing that talent and intelligence can be developed through effort and learning.

- Believing that mistakes are a part of learning and that failure is an opportunity for learning and growth.

- Believing that failure is a temporary setback and not permanent feedback to ability and talent.

- Embracing challenges and change as opportunities.

- Openly receiving constructive feedback from other people for the purpose of furthering learning and development.

- Viewing constructive feedback as a valuable resource of information.

- Viewing the success of other people as a source of information and inspiration.

By opening your mind and imagining the possibilities, you can find fulfillment in not just your financial life but in your life as an entirety.

Developing a growth mindset is not something that is innately ingrained in every human being. It is something that you have to work on and the best way to do so is to develop habits that will encourage you to think differently and adaptively. Such habits include:

- Developing your mission statement. Success is a personal and individualized process. Therefore, if you would like to be financially free you have to know how this is meaningful to you and what financial success means to you on an individual basis.

- Being goal oriented. You need to be clear on what you want out of your future and then work diligent in your effort to earn it.

- Continually learning and seeking new experiences. This allows you to broaden your horizons and gain you more experiences to shape your mind into one that is forward-thinking.

- Taking action. You will not get any results by sitting on the couch and dreaming about it. Successful people know this and get up and do something about earning the results that they would like.

- Being health conscious. The body and mind that you have now what you will have for as long as you remain on Earth. Eat right, exercise daily, keep hydrated and keep looking to keep both your body and mind fit enough to enable you to accomplish your goals of financial freedom. Financial freedom will elude you if either of these things start to fail you.

- Being self-disciplined. Successful people have mastered themselves so that they can control their actions and thoughts.

You cannot be dragged by your wants and desires and expect to be successful in your pursuit of financial security and independence.

Trading Options to Gain Financial Freedom

Trading options has the great potential to be a form of passive income. This is the complete opposite to active income, which is what most people engage in. Active income is one where a person invests time in exchange for money.

Passive income allows you to still enjoy your time as you dictate while earning money. It comes to you on automatic even while you sleep. While it usually takes time, effort and maybe monetary input at the beginning, over the long-term, if done right, you can sustain the lifestyle you want if you put forth that investment now.

Passive income:

- Gives you the platform to gain financial stability, security and independence.

- Gives you the freedom to do whatever you wish with your time without the worry of sustaining your financial life.

- Gives you the freedom to pursue the career, hobbies and other activities you love and enjoy rather than having to trade your time for money.

- Allows you to secure your financial future, thus getting rid of your worry, stress and anxiety in that department.

- Gives you the flexibility to live and work from anywhere in the world, typically. The bonus of this means you get to travel if that is a pursuit you would like to take on while still earning.

- Trading options can give you the benefits listed above and thus, light the way to your financial freedom.

Chapter 2 How Options Prices are Determined

P ricing is a complex subject when it comes to options trading. Not only is the price of an option based on the value of the asset, there are other external factors that have influence.

As an options trader, you want to make sure that you maximize your efforts to make a profit. Learning how to determine the prices you should pay for options is one of the basic ways that you can ensure that your yield is as high as it can be. You do not want to be stiffed by paying higher premiums than you should.

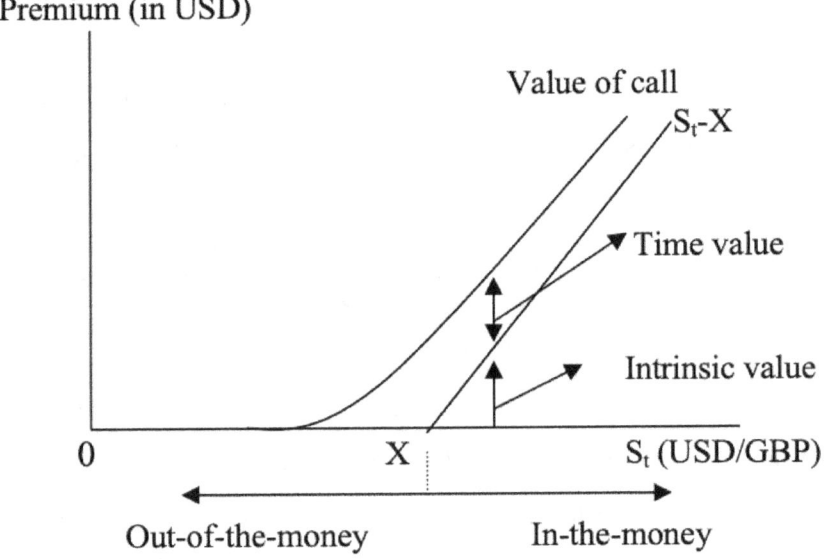

Pricing of options are determined by several factors.

The Value of the Asset

The effect this has on options prices is straightforward. If the value of this asset goes down, then exercising the option to sell becomes more valuable while the right to buy is become less valuable.

On the other hand, if the value increases, the right to sell it becomes less valuable while the right to buy it becomes more appealing due to this increase.

The Intrinsic Value

When an options trader pays a premium, this sum represents two values. The premium is made up of the intrinsic value, which is the current value of the option and the potential increase in value that this option can obtain over time. This potential increase over time is known as the time value.

The intrinsic value is how much money the option is currently worth. It represents what the buyer would receive if he or she decided to exercise the option at the current time.

Intrinsic value is calculated by determining the difference in the current price of an asset and a strike price of the option.

For an option to have an intrinsic value of zero, the option must be out of money. Therefore, the buyer would not exercise the option because this would result in a loss. The common strategy here is allowing the option to expire so that no pay off is made. As a result, the intrinsic value results in nothing to the buyer.

For a buyer to be in the money, the intrinsic value has to be greater than the premium to increase the value of the option. This place the buyer in a position to make a profit. The intrinsic value of for in the money for call options and put options are calculated slightly different. The formulas are as follows:

In the money call options

Price of Asset - Strike Price = Intrinsic Value

In the money put option

Strike Price - Price of Asset = Intrinsic Value

Intrinsic Value Formula

$$\text{Intrinsic Value of Business} = \frac{FCFE_1}{(1+r)^1} + \frac{FCFE_2}{(1+r)^2} + \cdots + \frac{FCFE_n}{(1+r)^n} + \frac{\text{Terminal Value}}{(1+r)^n}$$

$$\text{Intrinsic Value of Stock} = \frac{\text{Intrinsic Value Business}}{\text{No. of Outstanding Shares}}$$

The Time Value

This value is the additional amount an investor is willing to contribute to the premium of an option in addition to the intrinsic value. This willingness stems from the belief that an option will increase in value before the expiration date reaches. Typically, an investor is only willing to put forth this extra amount if the option expires months away. There would be little to no change in the value of an option in a few days.

The time value is calculated by finding the difference between the intrinsic value of an option and the premium. The formula looks like this:

Option Premium - Intrinsic Value = Time Value

Therefore, the total price of an option premium follows this formula:

Intrinsic Value + Time Value = Option Premium

Both time value and intrinsic value help traders understand the value of what they are paying for if they decide to purchase an option. While the intrinsic value represents the worth of the option if the buyer were to exercise it at the current time, the time value represents the possible future value before or on the expiration date. These two values are important because they help traders understand the risk versus the reward of considering an option.

Volatility

This describes how likely a price change will occur during a specified amount of time on the financial market. If a financial market is nonvolatile then the prices change very slowly or remain totally unaffected over a specific amount of time. Volatile markets, on the other hand, have fast-changing prices over short periods of time.

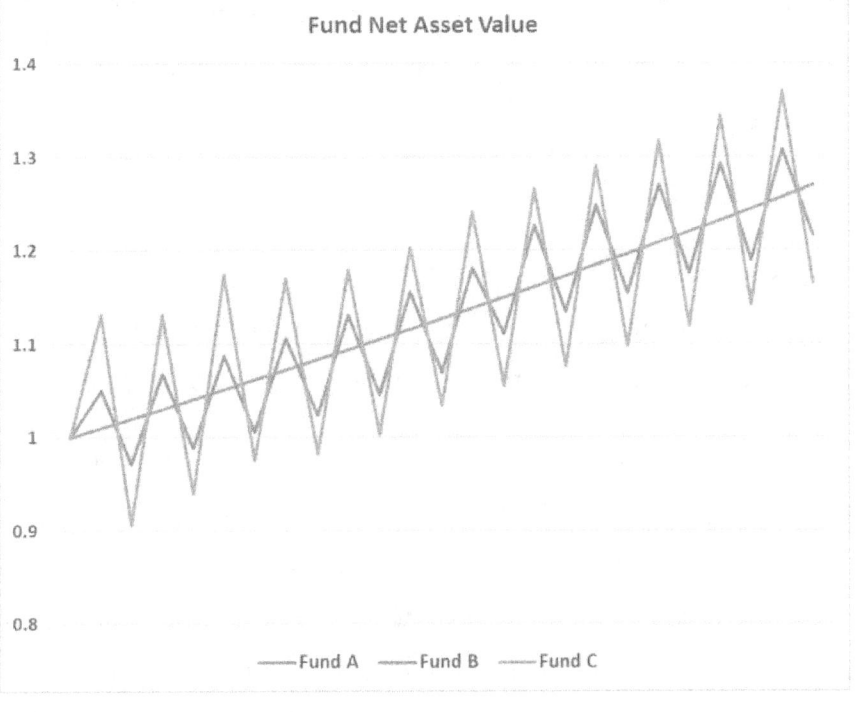

Option traders can make use of a financial market's volatility to get a higher yield for their investment in the future. Options traders normally avoid slow-changing financial markets because these non-volatile markets often mean that no potential profit is available to the trader. Therefore, option traders thrive on volatility even though volatility increases the risk of option trading. As a result, an options trader needs to know how to read the financial market correctly to know which options are likely to yield the highest returns. This ability comes with experience, continuous learning and keeping up to date on the happenings of the financial markets.

There are many factors that affect the volatility of a financial market. These factors include politics, national economics and news reports.

Options traders typically use one of two options strategies to gain the best yield from volatile markets. They are called straddle strategy and the strangle strategy.

Interest Rates

Most people are familiar with the term interest rates. Interest rates apply to mortgages bank accounts and more. Interest rates as it applies to option trading is slightly different from the common variations.

The interest rate is defined as the percentage of a particular rate for the use of money lent over a period of time. This interest rate of an option has different effects on the call option and put option. The premiums for call options rise when interest rates rise and fall when interest rates fall. The effect is the opposite on puts options. The premiums for put options fall when interest rates rise and rise when interest rates fall.

Interest rates affect the time value of options no matter what category they fall in!

You will come across the term risk-free interest rate many times in your study of options trading. This is described as the return made on an investment with no loss of capital. This is a misleading term because all investments carry some level of risk, no matter how minute. This more serves as a parameter in options pricing models such as the Black-Scholes Model to determine the premium that should be paid.

Dividends

Dividends are distributions of portions of a company's profit at a specified period. This distribution must be decided and managed by the board of directors of a company. It is paid to a particular class of shareholders. Dividends can be distributed in the form of cash, shares of stock and other types of property. Exchange-traded funds and mutual funds also pay out dividends.

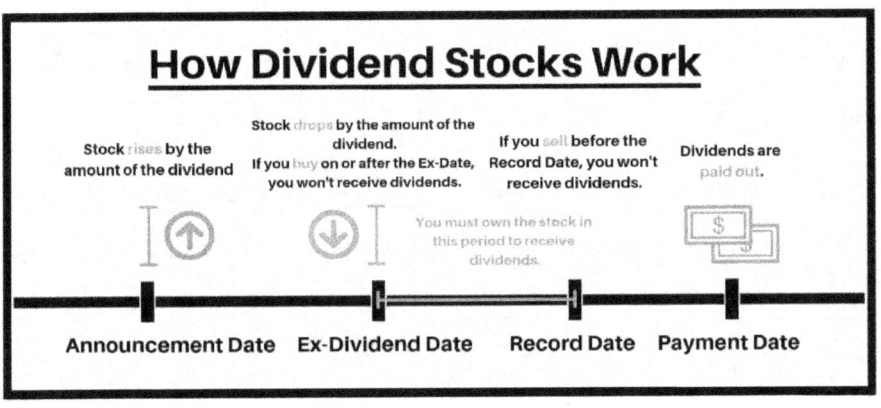

As it relates to options trading, options do not actually pay dividends. However, the associated assets attached to that option can have them and thus, options trader can receive those dividends if he or she exercises that option and takes ownership of those particular assets. While both call and put options can be affected by the presence of dividends of the associated asset, this effect on the types of options is widely varied. While the presence of dividends makes call options less expensive due to the anticipation of a drop-in price, it makes put options more expensive because the price will be decreased by the amount of the dividend.

Chapter 3 How to Get Started in Options Trading

Options trading has helped many investors to manage and grow their portfolio. Through the knowledge of options trading, many investors have protected their asset portfolio from risks and increase returns. The key is to know how to play the game and win.

Even though we have seen and heard the stories of many people how have become enormously successful in options trading, many people still have fears. You don't have to be afraid of trading in options because of the underlying risks. As with all investments, there is an amount of risk. To lower the risks, you have to know what you are doing. When you have better clarity about what you're doing, it limits your risks and set you on the path of success. By learning the basics of options trading and using the basic strategies to maximize your gains, you'll find yourself doing well in options trading. As a beginner options trading, what you have to do is to make sure you calm yourself down and start taking steps to begin your trade.

Options Trading Account

Your trading account is where all options trading activities will be done. Basically, an options trading account is a system or platform used by an investor to purchase and buy financial securities such as stocks, index and many others. The trading account is held by the brokerage firm and used to manage trading activities on your behalf. With an online trading account, you can hold cash, stocks, and another type of securities.

Technology has made it easy for managing trading accounts. To start using your trading account, you must first of all fund it. Many people think they can use a cheque from a friend fund their options trading account. Well, that is not allowed. Your bank account will be connected to the trading account. Through bank wire or transfer, you can transfer funds into the brokerage account through your savings or checking accounts.

Another factor to consider is a tax. Your trading account can be taxable or tax-deferred like a 401 (k). You can also decide if your trading account will be a taxable or simply a nonretirement account. You can choose to open an individual account or brokerage account for your business to trade. These are just forming of trading account, but there are two main types based on their functionality: margin and cash trading account.

Margin vs. Cash Trading Account

Margin Trading Account: A margin account is simply a brokerage account that provides you with a line of credit to buy options, stocks and other securities. Are you planning on using leverage for your trading? Through a margin trading account, you can borrow money to buy stocks or options. This gives you a form of leverage if you don't have cash at hand to purchase securities.

What you need to know about margin trading account is that all margins come with an interest. Each money borrowed to you for trading has an interest associated with it. That means for each that trade you are successful with, the brokerage account has to deduct taxes, fees and interests used in purchasing the securities.

The typical rate is 2% over the prime interest rate. An Intraday Margin Account, for instance, works on 4: 1 leverage ratio. That means for every amount of equity that you have; you will be granted access to credit four (4) times that amount. Let's say that you have a cash amount of $ 1,000 through an intra margin account you can borrow as much as $ 4,000 for your trading activities.

Cash Trading Account: A trading account deals with only cash. There is no line of credits for you to borrow the securities you deem feasible for you. All trading transactions in your account will be done via the cash you have transferred into the trading account via your savings or checking bank account. This account means you have no form of leverage for all trading decisions. For instance, when you placed $ 1,000 into your cash trading account, the only money available for you to spend in buying and trading securities will be that $ 1,000.00. If you don't close any position in your trading account, you will not have any line of credit to provide you with purchasing power. The settlement date for cash accounts varies, but they can be as short as the day of the transaction and following one.

Steps to Open a Trading Account

1. Providing Personal Information

To open a trading account, the brokerage firm will require you to provide certain personal financial information. This financial information helps the broker to track, manage and handle your account. You need to be careful you provide the right details to facilitate smooth trading activities. The sign-up process for a brokerage account varies from one broker to another, but the personal information required to run the account is almost the same.

2. Providing Additional Information

The following the information to be provided: Your legal name, email address, social security number, employment status, approximate annual income, and others. Some brokers want to know your experience level in trading underlying securities like stocks, index funds, and options.

Are you a registered broker-dealer? Are you managing a brokerage account on behalf of an individual or an institution?

Are you a shareholder in a company assigned to manage the brokerage account for the company? All this additional information will be asked to enable the broker to tailor their services to you. A special disclosure obligation will also be provided to authenticate and protect the information provided.

3. Idle Cash Management

If you have idle cash in your brokerage account, how will it be managed? Your broker would want to know how you intend to handle or manage the account. For example, you have invested and earned $ 16,500 worth of money. You have decided to trade in other securities with $ 10,000, what would you like the idle 6,500 to do? You might want to instruct the broker to push it into interest-bearing accounts such as treasury funds, mutual funds or even the money markets. 4. Trading Account Suitability

There are various kinds of trading styles. Your broker would want to know the best way you want to handle risk and manage trading activities. It is the goal of the broker to know the customer and provide the best support and services to be successful in trading activities. Some of the trading style can be: aggressive growth (more risk-taking in volatile securities), Simple Growth (gain money while preserving original capital), Income Risk Level (using income generate from profits for further trading) and Conservative (capital preservation and using the account of only one thing to protect existing assets).

5. Signing Account Opening Agreement

Before the trading account is opened, the broker would ensure that you sign and approve all the information provided. You might want to review all the information provided as well as read the contract statement to know the terms, policies and conditions used by the broker in managing the trading account. Once you are done, you can then confirm to agree with the terms for the trading contract. An electronic signature, print & sign or mail & sign will be used.

7 Easy Steps to Start Options Trading

To begin options trading, the following are some things to get started with:

1. Initial Preparation

2. Choosing an online broker

3. Finding your options trading niche

4. Finding option trades opportunities

5. Planning individual trades

6. Risk and money management

7. Monitoring your trades

Initial Preparation

It all starts with your mindset. Before you begin options trading, you have to make sure that you have the right mindset of successful options traders. Are you afraid of risk or you are risk lover? What is your attitude towards winning and losing? What is your approach to trading in the financial market? Analyze yourself and see if options trading for you, looking at your deep-seated values.

You also need to develop a trading plan. You've got to develop a trading plan that outlines your entry and exit strategy. If you don't have a long-term plan for options trading, chances are that you will give up in the first three or six months. Have profits targets and income ceiling to hit for options trading.

You also need to develop an action plan to get you doing. You have to make a to-do list for your options trading. How many hours will you be dedicated to the craft and focusing to increase your gains in options trading? How many minutes per day will you dedicate to studying the market and learning about options trading?

Choosing an Online Options Trader

To buy and sell options, you need a verified, licensed and approved online broker. There is a lot of options broker out there catering for different needs and goals of people. The key is to be clear about your options trading plan and then decided on the type of options broker that will help you to get there. You need to check whether the broker has been approved. You also want to look at the customer service levels of the broker. If you can, call them to ask about brokerage fees, commissions and service levels. Be clear about what you need so that it makes it easy for you to make your inquiry and find the best online broker that can meet your needs.

The best online brokers are focused on serving their customers. They have the best interest of their customers at heart. Therefore, their services are well-structured to meet their needs and help them to achieve their goals. They also have a high-quality trading platform with tools, analysis and guides to help make your options trading fun and exciting.

Finding Your Options Trading Niche

What is your options trading niche? Which kind of trade do you want to focus on? The type of options you choose can be based on your trading plan. Everything flows and revolves around your trading plan. This is why you must invest a considerable amount of time to develop a good trading plan that helps to define your options trading niche. Even if you choose to be a stock options trader, you have to clarify your position. Do you want to be a long-term investor, swing trader, day trader, value investor or a technical analyst? Would you want to be a net buyer of options or a net seller of options? Usually, a net buyer of options focus on using strategies such as long calls, long straddles, long puts, long strangles and many more.

As a net buyer of options, you play at the debit side of the game, reducing the amount of risk in each trade and increasing your gains. A net seller of options is rather focused on using strategies such as short put, short calls, short straddles, short strangles and much more. In this game, you focus on receiving premiums for placing a trade and capping your risk every trade to maximize gains. You have to choose how to play the options trading and then become an expert in one particular area.

Finding Options Trading Opportunities

Once you have defined your niche, the next step is to begin to find opportunities that fit your area of expertise. Finding opportunities have to do with working with your options broker. The main job of your options broker is to know your trading plan and then help you spot opportunities that are in align with your trading plan.

You might also choose to trade in companies that you are comfortable or understand what there are doing. That depends on your trading plan. But to find good options trading opportunities you have to make good use of your trading account and then also dedicate a certain amount of time to study the trade.

Chapter 4 Reasons Why Options Trading Is Better Than Stock Trading

Options trading has been the focal point of much discussion of ongoing years. Is it risky? Would we be able to go bankrupt? For sure, options as a type of subsidiary instrument is unmistakably more perplexing If you don't see how it works and how to use it properly.

In this part, I will exhibit 5 reasons why options trading is, in reality, superior to anything stock trading to scatter the well-established legends of how perilous options trading is. We should recollect this: Options trading is hazardous just when you don't get it.

1. **Variable Leverage**

The influence that options give you is maybe the principle motivation behind why individuals incline toward options trading in any case. The excellence of influence in options, not at all like in prospects trading, is that it is VARIABLE!

You could take on more impact for more peril or lesser significance for lesser risk by picking choices of different strike costs and also end month. All things considered, the more out of the cash choices, the higher the impact and the more in the cash choices, the lower the impact.

Influence cuts the two different ways. This is the reason the excellence of control in options trading is that it enables you to do similar trades with a lot lesser money, all things considered, you could primarily utilize just money you can bear to and plan to lose in any fizzled trade for every alternative, so influence really help you control your misfortunes!

2. Low Capital Requirement

Apple Inc., AAPL, is trading at $295.36 today, which implies it takes $29,536 to buy 100 offers today. In any case, AAPL's at the money call options costs just something like $715 to control the profits on that equivalent 100 offers of Apple!

3. Bet Downwards Without Margin

To benefit from a downwards proceed onward a stock in stock trading, you could short the stock which causes edge. In trading options, all you have to do to wager on stock going down is to BUY your options with no margin required by any means. It's hard to believe, but it's true, buying put options for the benefit to drawback works precisely equivalent to buying call options for the benefit to the upside. There is no compelling reason to possess the stock previously, and there is no requirement for the edge!

4. Multi-Directional Profits

In stock trading, you conceivably advantage when the stock goes toward the way you need it to. There is no genuine method to profit in the two circumstances simultaneously, and there is no down to earth approach to help if the expense of the stock doesn't move. In any case, in choices exchanging, such multi-directional benefits are possible! Such is the unadulterated charm of choices philosophies which colossally manufactures your chances of winning in alternatives exchanging versus stock exchanging!

5. Play Banker

Weary of continually being at the player's side of the table? In options trading, you could change slightly to the investor's side of the table and do what market producers do by selling options to individuals who are needs to take the bottom of the player! At the point when the players lose, as they frequently do, you get the opportunity to keep the wager as a benefit only like a genuine investor! Just options trading has the "wager," which you had the opportunity to, and it is known as "outward esteem."

Chapter 5 Basics Options Strategies Going Long

The strategy for profiting from going long on a call or put option is simple. The industry is full of naysayers that downplay this basic strategy; however, the reality is you can definitely earn profits in this way. That is buying or selling individual options, be they the call or put variety. The key to success when doing this type of trading is to stay on top of it and don't buy options on a whim. You need a good reason to buy a call or a put option by itself, and that means paying attention to the financial news.

Day Trading and Options

This is just an aside but watching the movement of a stock price over the course of a single day can provide opportunities to ride a short-term trend in price and profit handsomely. Rising and falling share prices are magnified in the price of the option, so when the share price goes up a few tens of cents, you might profit by $65 or $75 in a single day.

But be aware that the rules for day trading apply to options as well. In order to be a day trader approved by your broker in the United States, you need to have a margin account and it needs to have $25,000 deposited in the account. Since options trading often takes place on the level of tens or hundreds of dollars at a time, the vast majority of beginning options traders are not going to be looking to be a day trader.

The rule you need to be aware of is if you make four-day trades over a five-day period, that means you will be labeled a pattern day trader. To keep your account open, you'd have to fund it with $25,000. So, this is a situation that you are probably going to want to avoid. In order to avoid being pulled under by this, simply limit the number of day trades to 3 per week.

Remember that the five-day rule means five consecutive trading days, so weekends don't count. If you made a day trade on Friday, the following Monday, that day trade still counts against you.

Call Options Basic Strategy

The basic strategy behind making profits with call options is to buy low and sell high. You can profit from this strategy riding a single day's price movements or by "swing trading" the option over the course of one or more days, meaning that you will hold the option overnight. You are not going to hold the option until expiration unless you have the intention of buying the stock.

The time to sell the option is the point at which you have made an acceptable level of profits. You should set this level beforehand so that you are not letting the emotions of the moment rule your decisions. It's not uncommon to make $50 or $100 profits in a few days or even in a single day off of one option contract, but many traders get dollar signs in their eyes – they get overcome with greed – and as a result, they hold their positions too long. That can mean lost profits, defeat by time decay, or even seeing the option wiped out.

One lesson that you are going to learn is that options prices can fluctuate dramatically. This is because the underlying stock is 100 shares. So, a small change in the stock price is magnified by 100 for your investment in the option. Using a one-to-one pricing relationship for the sake of simplicity, if the price of the stock moves up by a mere 45 cents, the price of the option will go up by $45. On the other hand, if it drops by 30 cents, the price of the option would drop $30.

Although the situation of using one-to-one pricing is not realistic it's pretty clear that small price changes in stock mean significant price changes in your investment.

The key to success with trading options is to have a trading plan that you follow, and which has specific rules.

One skill you are going to need to develop when it comes to call options is the ability to read stock charts. There are three basic skills that I recommend you have:

- Learn how to read and interpret candlestick charts.
- Learn how to use moving averages.
- Learn how to use and interpret Bollinger bands.

Let's give a few specific examples so that you will have some practical advice for the situation. You can trade index funds like the Dow Jones Industrial Average (trade options on DIA), the S & P 500 (trade options on SPY), or the NASDAQ (trade options on QQQ). These index funds are very sensitive to general economic and political news. So, if you see that a good jobs report has come out, that is a good signal to get in on one or more of these funds. In fact, it's often worth the risk to get in on options for these index funds the day before. Then you can wake up and see the results. It's going to be possible to double an investment overnight. Since you are not day trading, in that case, it's a simple matter to exit your positions for a profit. But keep in mind, there is a risk as well if it works against you (we will discuss strategies to use to cover both movements). If you buy a call but the early indication is a market sell-off, then get rid of the put first thing when the market opens.

This is a good example of why open interest is important to look at. If you were to buy an option on something with a small level of open interest, you might not be able to get rid of your options before the put lost a lot of money. With something that is very heavily traded like SPY, however, it's a sure bet that you can unload the put quickly.

You also want to pay attention to news about specific companies. For example, if there is news coming out in the early morning hours that the government is going to investigate the social media companies, that is a good indication that going long on a put option would be a reasonable strategy. Conversely, recently, the FTC announced a settlement with Facebook, and this sent the stock soaring.

Reading the Charts

As an options trader, you are going to have to learn how to read charts. The first thing to do is look up candlestick patterns so that you can recognize when a trend reversal might be coming. Candlestick patterns are not absolute rules or truth-tellers, they are an indicator. So, you take the candlestick charts into consideration and use the entirety of the information that you have available to make your decisions.

The candlesticks are going to be colored green or red. If a candlestick is green, it's a "bullish" candlestick. That means that over the period of interest, the closing price had risen to a larger higher than the opening price. By itself, it does not tell you where the price is headed. For a bullish candlestick, the top of the candle is the price at the end of the trading session, and the bottom of the body is the price at the start.

Each candlestick has "wicks" that come out of the top and bottom of the candlestick. The top wick gives you the high price for the time interval. The bottom candlestick gives you the low price of the time interval.

If a candlestick is red, that is a "bearish" candlestick. In that case, this means that the closing price was lower than the opening price. So, the top of the body is the opening price in this case, and the bottom of the body is the closing price (the price closed lower than it opened at). The meaning of wicks is the same.

That said, here are the general rules for entering and exiting trades.

For beginners, I have to say get ready for the ride. If you are thin-skinned, this kind of trading is going to put you on pins and needles. As you know, stock prices do not follow a steady curve, they move up and down a lot. And as we have mentioned several times, a small move in share price which really isn't all that significant can have a big impact on options prices. It's not uncommon to get into a trade and see your option lose $75 or $100 over the course of a couple of hours, and then see it rise to a $50 or $100 profit a few hours later. So, this is not something for the faint of heart to get involved with.

But to avoid panic, you should rely on the indicators to help you make your decisions rather than relying on emotion.

The second big tool you need to use in your trading is the moving average. I like to use a 9-period case. This will be for an exponential moving average. Then for the long one, I will use twenty periods. Again, it will be an exponential moving average on the same chart. Moving averages average out the stock prices to give you smooth curves that show the overall price trend. Using two moving averages allows you to get signals when a trend is going to reverse. This actually works quite well in practice. The signal for a reversal is when the moving averages cross.

If a short period moving average crosses above a long period moving average, this is taken to be a signal of a coming uptrend. So, in my case, I look for the 9-period moving average to cross above the 20-period moving average. This can be used to either reinforce your conviction that you should say in the trade or to enter a trade if you are looking to take advantage of a coming price movement (for call options).

You can also add a tool called the RSI to your charts, which is the relative strength indicator. This tells you if a stock is overbought or oversold. If the RSI is 70 or above, then the stock is considered to be overbought, and that can be a good time to exit a long call position. If the RSI is 30 or below, this is "oversold", and so it can be a good time to enter a long position for call options. I take the RSI with a grain of salt because I've seen it indicate overbought conditions which were then followed by continually rising prices, all too often. But it's one thing that you can consider looking at.

Finally, there are the Bollinger bands. These give you a moving average along with the standard deviation both above and below the moving average. If you are going to use this, the main reason would be to establish levels of support and resistance. A level of support is a low-price level that the stock is unlikely to break below over a short time period. A level of resistance is the maximum price you are likely to see for the stock over a short time period. These are guidelines, a stock might suddenly break out of a range at any time.

Chapter 6 Option Risk and Reward

Money management is only included in the trading plan by about one-tenth of all private traders. Just because a trader does not have a lot of capital does not mean that he cannot apply the principles of money management. Many traders are of the opinion that these ideas can only be used by large asset managers and institutions.

Money management also implies that the potential risk, considering the preferences of the trader, is set in relation to the expected profit. The goal is to set a desirable yield rate and then minimize the associated risk. Trading generally requires four decisions:

1. Buy/sell (system or strategy)?

2. Which security is traded?

3. How many contracts or shares of value are traded?

4. What is the share of capital risked on a trade?

The first decision is about the trading process itself without considering money management. The other three decisions involve maximizing profit and minimizing risk directly. The foundations of risk and reward should be considered from the start in the development of a trading system and must become an integral part of the system.

If a trader works profitably right from the start and has thus increased his trading capital, then he cannot be ruined by four losses (as long as his bet remains the same). Although the number of consecutive losses that would lead to ruin increases with time, so does the likelihood of multiple losses follow one another. The following formula calculates the probability of ultimate ruin (WR) over time:

$$WR = (1-VT / 1 + VT) AH$$

VT stands for the trader's advantage (percentage winners - percent losers), and AH is the initial trading units. If the initial capital of a trader is $ 20,000 and his bet per trade is $ 5,000 then AH = 4. The following example calculates the probability of ultimate ruin:

Total Capital$ 20,000Total Capital$ 20,000

Deployment$ 5,000Deployment$ 2,500

Advantage of the Trade10%Trades' Advantage 10%

Chance of Ruin44.8%Chance of Ruin20.1%

Total Capital$ 20,000Total Capital$ 20,000

Bet$ 2,000Bet$ 1,000

Advantage of the Trade10%Advantage of the Trade 10%

Chance of Ruin13.4%Chance of Ruin1.8%

These numbers apply only when you trade one contract at a time. With changing contract numbers, the risk of ruin changes dramatically. Moreover, these calculations assume that, in the case of a profit, the amount is always the same and corresponds to the loss in the negative case. As mentioned above, the risk of ruin is determined by the percentage of winners, the ratio between winners and losers, and the size of the bet. So far, we have disregarded the relationship between winners and losers. In real life, most successful trading systems score less than 50% winners and win-loss ratios above 1.2.

The risk of ruin is an interesting indicator, but it does not give much insight into how to use or manage capital efficiently. For self-preservation, it is best not to put everything on one card. If you choose your bets well and follow a system with a positive bias, the risk of ruin is very low.

The Capital Allocation Model

Now you know the tools you need to understand our capital allocation model. First, we'll show how capital is allocated to a one-market portfolio using a small selection of data. Later, we will apply the same approach to a two-market portfolio.

As you know, our goal is to maximize profit while minimizing risk. This goal must be achieved without exceeding the limits of justifiable risk. To reach the goal, we need to know how much capital is to be allocated to each market and what number of contracts should be traded. In this model, capital is calculated from the market value of the account, the average monthly returns, and the market risk. The market value is simply the starting capital with which we begin our trading. In these examples, the returns do not add up; we use the initial capital for all calculations. The average monthly income is the capital that we can expect to gain from our system. Market risk is the amount we can lose per day on a trade. Asset managers use a variety of metrics to assess market risk:

- Mean Range: The average of the ranges of the last three to 50 Days, which is converted into a monetary amount in US $. For example, if the average spread is 40 points for the Swiss franc over the past 10 days and the Swiss franc is $ 12.50, the market risk is $ 500. The likely amount of market movement is the average spread of the last x days. This does not always have to be right, but the capital allocation model needs to be built on certain probabilities.

- The average change in closing prices: The average change in closing prices over the last three to 50 days says more about the risk, as this value indicates the expected risk if the position is held.

- Mean change in positive closing prices versus negative closing prices: the average change in the negative closing prices over a period suggests the risk of holding a long position.

- The standard deviation of closing prices: The standard deviation of the closing prices gives a more accurate picture of the risk, as the daily deviation is displayed with a probability of 68%. This calculation is a bit more complex, but it does not cause any problems with the computers available today.

In whatever way we measure the risk, it is the most important variable to watch and the most important component of the capital allocation model.

A Market Portfolio

Whether the system trades futures or stocks makes no difference. Before we can allocate capital, the average monthly income and market risk must be determined on the basis of a contract. We also need to determine how much of our capital we are willing to risk per trade. But we cannot know that yet, because that's exactly what we want to find out.

Cumulating of Results

Cumulating means here the process of capital allocation based on the current portfolio or deposit value. The current portfolio value results from the start-up capital as well as the already completed positive and negative trades. When it comes to large sums of money, accumulation is very good: the capital invested increases or decreases depending on the current value of the deposit. If a trading plan is successful, then each trade will be given more capital; but if it is bad, then there is less capital available for each trade. Note that we have found that cumulating is very good when it comes to large sums. This limitation stems from the belief that the allocation should not be extended until the seed capital of smaller accounts has not been at least doubled or tripled. Even good systems can crash after a series of wins, and if a smaller account does not cumulate, there is still some capital left for bad times.

If accumulation is of interest to you (and it should, if you have significant sums of money), then you can build it into the capital allocation model with a small change. In the formula, do not use seed capital as total capital (GK), but use the current value of the deposit.

Chapter 7 Understanding Options Risks

Options trading process does carry some risks with it. Understanding these risks and taking mitigating steps will make you not just a better trader but a more profitable one as well. A lot of trader's love options trading because of the immense leverage that this kind of trading affords them. Should an investment work out as desired, then the profits are often quite high. With stocks, you can expect returns of between 10%, 15%, or even 20%. However, when it comes to options, profit margins in excess of 1,000% are very possible.

Basically, these kinds of trades are very possible due to the nature and leverage offered by options. A savvy trader realizes that he or she is able to control an almost equivalent number of shares as a traditional stock investor but at a fraction of the cost. Therefore, when you invest in options, you can spend a tiny amount of money to control a large number of shares. This kind of leverage limits your risks and exposure compared to a stock investor.

As an investor or trader, you should never spend more than 3% to 5% of your funds in any single trade. For instance, if you have $10,000 to invest, you should not spend more than $300 to $500 on any one trade. Also, as a trader, you are not just mitigating against potential risks but are also looking to take advantage of the leverage. This is also known as gaining a professional trader's edge. While it is crucial to reduce the risk through careful analysis and selection of trades, you should also aim to make huge profits and enjoy big returns on your trades. There will always be some losses, and as a trader, you should get to appreciate this. However, your major goal as a trader should be to ensure that your wins are much, much larger than any losses that you may suffer.

All types of investment opportunities carry a certain level of risk. However, options trading carries a much higher risk of loss. Therefore, ensure that you have a thorough understanding of the risks and always be on the lookout. Also, these kinds of trades are very possible due to the nature and leverage offered by options. A savvy trader realizes that he or she is able to control an almost equivalent number of shares as a traditional stock investor but at a fraction of the cost. Therefore, when you invest in options, you can spend a tiny amount of money to control a large number of shares. This kind of leverage limits your risks and exposure compared to a stock investor.

Time Is Not on Your Side

You need to keep in mind that all options have an expiration date and that they do expire in time. When you invest in stocks, time is on your side most of the time. However, things are different when it comes to options. Basically, the closer that an option gets to its expiration, the quicker it loses its value and earning potential.

Options deterioration is usually rather rapid, and it accelerates in the last days until expiration. Basically, as an investor, ensure that you only invest dollar amounts that you can afford to lose. The good news though is that there are a couple of actions that you can take in order to get things on your side.

- Trade mostly in options with expiration dates that are within the investment opportunity

- Buy options at or very near the money

- Sell options any time you think volatility is highly priced

- Buy options when you are of the opinion that volatility is underpriced

- Prices Can Move Pretty Fast

Options are highly leveraged financial instruments. Because of this, prices tend to move pretty fast. Basically, options prices can move huge amounts within minutes and sometimes even seconds. This is unlike other stock market instruments like stocks that move in hours and days.

Small movements in the price of a stock can have huge implications on the value of the underlying stock. You need to be vigilant and monitor price movements often. However, you can generate profits without monitoring activity on the markets twenty-four hours a day.

As an investor or trader, you should seek out opportunities where chances of earning a significant profit are immense. The opportunity should be sufficiently robust so that pricing by seconds will be of little concern. In short, search for opportunities that will lead to large profits even when you are not accurate when selling.

When structuring your options, you should ensure that you use the correct strike prices as well as expiration months in order to cut out most of the risk. You should also consider closing out your trades well before expiration of options. This way, time value will not dramatically deteriorate.

Naked Short Positions Can Result in Substantial Losses

Anytime that your naked short option presents a high likelihood of substantial and sometimes even unlimited losses. Shorting put naked means selling stock options with no hedging of your position.

When selling a naked short, it simply implies that you are actually selling a call option or even a put option but without securing it using an option position, a stock or cash. It is advisable to sell a put or a call-in combination with other options or with stocks. Remember that whenever you short sell a stock, you are in essence selling borrowed stock. Sooner or later, you will have to return the stock.

Fortunately, with options, there is no borrowing of stock or any other security.

Chapter 8 Development of The Option

Options belong to the group of financial derivatives. These are standardized trading instruments. The price development of basic security is the measure for the later price. In the case of derivatives, equities, indices, currencies, or even the derivatives themselves may form the underlying. When traded on the stock exchange, investors most often encounter derivatives in the form of options or futures. These forms of investment are among the most traded products on the stock market. But what is it exactly, and how did the option develop until the speculative derivative emerged as the currently valid trading tool?

- Options are traded on the stock exchange

- The option is a variant of the derivative

- Derivatives may be based on different titles

- Basic title is authoritative for the later price

The classic option offers the right to trade a commodity at a price called the strike price. Both the acquisition (call) and the sale (put) may be considered. Trading does not constitute an obligation, which means that the trader does not need to buy or sell the stock or any other underlying asset. It is merely a matter of justifying the right to trade a commercial product at the pre-determined price at a later date. To acquire the option, the investor pays the seller, who is also called the writer, a premium, namely the option price; A call warrant thus includes securitization on the right to buy the underlying asset. If you trade the American variation, you, as a buyer, can exercise your option right at any time until the due date.

On the other hand, you can exercise your right in the European version only on the due date. In most circumstances, investors will only exercise the call or put if the price of the underlying at the time of maturity is above or below the base value. Otherwise, the investor should trade the security at a better price in the market. For Call and Put, there are the following profiles:

- Call: Purchase Option - Right to buy the underlying asset

- Put: Put option - Right to sell the underlying asset

- Long: Viewpoint Buyer - buyer position

- Short: Viewing Angle Seller - Verkaufspositon

Note: Buyers and Sellers refer to the option and not to the underlying asset.

The purchase warrant (call): set on rising prices

The above can best be described by way of example: An investor acquires a warrant of purchase from a bank, also known as an issuer, on a Siemens AG security. This has a base price of 109 euros. The option type is American in this case, and the term has been set to six months. The trader thus has the right to demand from the bank the delivery of the share of Siemens AG at the price of 109 euros. If the paper of Siemens AG is now listed at 120 euros after some time, it is worthwhile for the investor to buy the share at the price of 109 euros. However, should the Siemens share fall to 90 euros, it is cheaper for the investor to buy the security on the market. Therefore, he becomes the option right expire and buys the stock directly on the stock exchange.

However, it remains questionable whether this action also brings the investor a profit. The answer to this question depends primarily on how high the option premium was. Put the case, and the buyer paid a premium of five euros on the right to buy the paper by the due date for 109 euros. In the case of options expiration, the trader has at least made a loss of five euros. When making a purchase, however, he only makes a profit when the underlying asset rises above 109 euros plus the premium, i.e., to more than 114 euros. Under such circumstances, investors may be able to profit indefinitely from rising prices through such a warrant. If the price falls, the loss remains limited to the option premium.

How are warrant options different?

Both options, as well as warrants, are financial instruments with which future transactions are carried out. That's what they have in common with futures. Investors act in these transactions, so to speak, on the development of the option or the warrant. Because trade refers to a delimited period, these two derivatives are based on the same principle. The buyer of the call option speculates that the price of the underlying asset will rise within a specified period or until the due date. This puts the trader in the position to buy the underlying at a meager price. The investor makes the actual profit if he immediately resells the underlying asset in a favorably stored case at a higher value. Thus, he can strike the difference of the market value at the beginning of the legal transaction from the value on the due date.

In contrast, the seller of the call option speculates on a falling price. At the same time, he assumes that the buyer of the right does not avail himself of the opportunity to acquire the underlying asset. Thus, the seller earns a profit with the premium and the further retention of the underlying.

Options and Warrants - A Comparison

Options are standardized products. These are traded as contracts on the futures exchange. By contrast, warrants are among the securities. They are issued by the issuers (for example, the banks). However, the issuer does not usually speculate on a falling price. The issuers issue another warrant, which should have a contrary effect. Thus, the bank escapes the event of taking a risk as the price either falls or rises. The bank generates its profits from the commissions it receives for the issued warrants.

Warrant:

- is issued by an issuer who simultaneously sets the price
- the risk of insolvency borne by the dealer
- only long call or long put possible

Option:

- is provided by each market participant

- no risk, as the legal transactions are hedged

- the price is determined by the options exchange such as EUREX

- the conditions are standardized

- everything is possible such as long call, short call, long put, short put as well as combinations thereof

In principle, options and warrants are quite similar: both are forward transactions based on a previously established underlying asset. This value is also often called an underlying. For both variations, underlying of the following financial instruments may be available:

- Shares

- Currencies

- Indices

- Raw Materials

- Bonds

- Futures

Note: Options are highly transparent as their market value is published on the stock exchange every day. By contrast, warrants issued by the issuer have less transparency.

Trading Based on the Acquisition of Rights

The origin of these speculation products can be found in the Netherlands in the 17th century. At that time, the first tulips were bred there. Sometime after its introduction, the tulip became a popular flower in Holland. Eager flower growers set out to grow specific varieties that would bring in a lot of money. More and more interested flower lovers ordered the particular types from the florists, although they had not yet been brought to market. To give their action a firm reason, they paid for the tulips. In return, the florists offered to purchase a certain amount of tulip bulbs at a fixed price on a specific date. This created the basis for the first option.

In principle, the buyers did not want to invest their money at all, but their will was entirely directed to the exercise of the legal business. However, that could change if the tulips had lost significant value by the exercise date. In this case, the flower buyers were still obliged to purchase at the agreed price, and the tulip seller made a deal.

Note: The development of the option meant that the merchant had no choice during the time the options were created. He had to pick up the tulip bulbs at the previously agreed price, whether he wanted it or not. That could mean a huge win or bankruptcy for him.

The exercise right then and now

The development of the option lasted for a long time. In particular, the exercise obligation has changed over the years. In the early days, the buyer had to exercise his acquired right. If he had been authorized to buy 20 tulip bulbs at the price of 200 guilders, he could redeem them on the agreed date of purchase. If the tulips had risen in price, because the species and genus of this variety had suddenly gained in popularity, the dealer benefited from this advantage. He was then able to sell the tulip bulbs with a profit margin of one hundred percent.

If, however, the demand for this variety of tulips has declined in the meantime, then the tulip bulbs might have been only worth half the purchase date. Yet, even if they had not been worth anything, the businessman of the time had a duty to take off the tulips. The flower bulb buyer was not allowed to indicate that he wanted to renounce the trade. He had to pay the agreed amount of money to the florist and take worthless goods home. This circumstance has completely changed to this day. For the current options offered on the market, the investor can decide whether he wants to exercise his right to end the term or not. The investors enjoy these benefits today:

- if the financial product does not perform as desired, the highest possible loss is the risk of losing the option premium

- the default risk is therefore manageable since there is no commercial obligation

- Traders can still benefit from the better prices if they wish

Note: Financial products due to the transfer of a right now offer traders some advantages over other trading opportunities. If you find that your trade is different than you would like, you can now accept the loss of the option premium and let the transaction expire. You can calculate your risks in advance and act accordingly.

Advantages and disadvantages compared to warrants

Options have some advantages over warrants. This is especially true in terms of the risk involved. With both speculative instruments, traders with small capital can also trade through an account. The investor is not obliged to exercise. On the other hand, he can use the fact that the legal transaction has expired. Also, he has the opportunity to sell the financial derivative, in the American variant even before the maturity date.

Therefore, the investor does not necessarily have to have high financial reserves actually to invest in case of need. Options and warrants are tradable without having to buy the underlying asset. However, there is a unique feature in the warrants. These are rarely actually practiced. Its purpose serves above all the speculation on a profit advantage after a resale.

A lever can be used to multiply the profit of an option. However, it should also be noted that the risk of loss also increases if the price does not appreciate in the predicted way. In this case, traders can lose all their capital. The seller can always reap the option premium.

Both derivatives are used as a speculative instrument. On the other hand, they are an excellent way to hedge another position in the portfolio against loss. This is called hedging.

Chapter 9 Concepts Behind Options

A. Options are Derivatives

Financial instruments are a varied lot and are changing and growing all the time, sometimes rapidly. Everyone has heard about derivatives. Derivatives are simply financial instruments whose value depends on the value of some other instrument. The financial instruments commonly referred to are things like stocks, municipal bonds, notes, commercial bonds, ETF's, index funds, and so many more. Options are just another financial instrument, but they are a form of a derivative. That is, the value of the option depends on the value of the underlying financial instrument.

An option is a choice because you have the option to act on the contract or not, depending on your decisions and the market conditions. Normally, we would act on an option if the decision is in our favor and not if it is to our disadvantage. That is a strong argument for dealing in options. However, in most cases, you are not required to act on the contract, an action called execution of the option. You don't have to if you don't want to. On the other hand, if you buy an option to buy at the contract terms, the seller of that contract is required to sell under those terms. That part of options is a one-way street. Historically, only 10% of options are exercised, that is acted upon, 60% are traded before expiration and the remaining 30% expire worthless.

B. Trading in Options Has Both Risks and Rewards

Trading in options is not without risk, especially for new traders. It is remarkably easy to lose money trading in options. All it takes is a few bad decisions, which are frequently based on lack of understanding on the part of the investor or by not paying attention. We strongly recommend trading only with risk capital. That is, money you can afford to lose if things go bad. Don't trade in options with the rent money or the money set aside for the kid's college education.

C. Pick Your Own Trading Strategy

Your trading strategy can be speculative, income, or conservative. A speculative strategy is based on predicting the timing and amount of any movement in the price of the stock. A conservative strategy involves trading in a manner that protects against large losses for equities the investor owns. An income strategy is one under which you generate regular income above that from normal stock gains or dividends. We will cover these in due course.

Usually, options are based on common stocks. We will follow that custom, but options are available for many different instruments like ETF's and Stock Indices. It's just easier to understand with stocks.

D. Option Trading Uses its Own Vocabulary

When you understand a few basic concepts and some vocabulary, you will see that it is not all that complicated. However, you have to study not only the market, but the ins and outs of options trading, too. Now, some of the vocabulary may seem arcane, but it is the "lingo" of Wall

Street and is used by all traders and brokers everywhere. You will need to understand this vocabulary to understand the business of options trading.

E. Decide to Pay Attention

Remember, if you choose to trade in options, you have new opportunities but also new responsibilities. If you are holding options on a stock or other instrument, you must keep a close eye on it. There is nothing automatic about options. If you hold an option and it suddenly becomes very valuable, it is up to you to act on it. It will not act on its own, in fact, it may expire, and you will lose the premium cost and any value of the option. Under some circumstances, you may be assigned, which means you are required to act on the option. Apart from assignments, nobody is going to call you and ask you what you want to do. You have to follow it closely, but that is interesting and sometimes, exciting.

Chapter 10 Good Resources and Their Importance in Option Trading

Every successful investor says that research makes all the difference not only in options trading but trading in general. The better resources you have the more knowledge you will acquire. This is especially significant for learning as much as you can about underlying securities for example or to find as many details about the market that is constantly changing. Significance of the right source of information eventually becomes the key to your progress, even more, if the world of options trading is still new to you. We can say that there are two types of relevant resources for options trading. The first one includes traditional resources such as magazines, newsletters, and newspapers. The second type is newer, it has a variety of options and these kinds of resources are mostly referred to as online resources.

The Internet offers a variety of free content, which is why many investors see it as their first stop whenever they need some kind of information. Further technology development also had a huge impact on the amount of information, tools, and possibilities that a person can access so using apps for education and trading, in general, has become a common thing. In the following text, we will list some of the most relevant option trading resources divided into the categories we explained above.

Even though they are considered to be more traditional, magazines, newspapers, newsletters, are still popular for research, for both experienced investors and beginners on the market. It is useful to know that many newsletters offer paid services such as recommendations, picks, research of certain categories and other relevant information.

We will start with the magazines. Some of them such as Forbes is still one of the greatest and strongest magazines in the world for this matter. So, we have Fortune, Forbes, Consumer Money Adviser, Bloomberg BusinessWeek, Kiplinger's, and Fast Company as some of the most relevant magazines today.

Newspapers that you might find useful are the Financial Times, the Wall Street Journal, The Washington Post, Value Line, and Barron's.

As we already mentioned, newsletters often offer more detailed insight into the market matters. Some of the most recommended ones are ETF Trader, Market Watch Options Trader, The Proactive Fund Investor, Hulbert Interactive, The Technical Indicator, The Prudent Speculator, Dow Theory Forecasts, and Global Resources Trading

When it comes to online resources, they are probably the most frequent source of information for everything, not only for options trading. However, it is possible to find numerous websites that offer research that is up to date. Many of these analyses and other useful data can be found for free.

Technology development made many things easier with trading. Many apps have emerged and enabled investors to keep a close track of their investments at all times. It is important to know that there are apps that are not only for investment but for brokerage companies too. In the following text, you can find some of the investment apps that are most frequently used and that have excellent feedback.

How to avoid costly mistakes

Losing profit is not something that you want as an investor since the main purpose of options trading is to make money not the other way around. To do so, some tips can help you avoid mistakes that can be costly.

First of all, don't invest more capital than you are ready to lose. Keep in mind that trading options don't go without risks. There aren't any guarantees that the propositions that you'll face with will gain you anything and your decisions are based on the hunch. Furthermore, if you don't have good timing and your hunch isn't right, you can lose the entire investment, not only the cash you were expecting to earn. The best way to avoid this kind of scenario is to start small. It is recommended that you use no more than 15 percent of your total portfolio on options trading.

The second tip that you should be aware of at all times is that good research gets the job done. If somebody says that it is a good idea to invest in options and you rush in and make an order without thinking it through, once more, you can lose more than you could earn. You should make your own research and decide based on facts before you start trading.

There is another thing that you should be mindful of. No matter the strategy you choose for options trading, you should always try to adjust it to the current condition on the market. Not all strategies work in all environments which is why you must be up to date with circumstances in the world of finance and you have to adapt accordingly.

Without a proper exit strategy, it is useless to talk about successful business in options trading. You need to make a plan that you will follow through regardless of your emotions. Rational decisions are the main factor in trade, being emotional and making fast decisions out of rage or spite or feeling of insecurity can only make things worse. Stick to the plan you figured before you started trading because it should have both downside and upside points along with the timeframe for its execution. Just like you shouldn't let negative feelings influence your decision making, you shouldn't allow the feeling of over-confidence in gaining large profits pull you back from the path you have set for yourself.

When it comes to risks, there is no need to take more risks than necessary, which means that the level of risk should be as big as your comfort with it. Level of risk tolerance is different for everyone; it is an individual think and only the investor himself can set its limit. Try to estimate that level and then choose all further actions accordingly. It is the safest premise to base your decisions on without being too insecure about every choice you make.

Chapter 11 Analyzing Mood Swing in the Market

The market is a chaotic place with a number of traders vying for dominance over one another. There are a countless number of strategies and time frames in play and at any point, it is close to impossible to determine who will emerge with the upper hand. In such an environment, how is it then possible to make any money? After all, if everything is unpredictable, how can you get your picks right?

Well, this is where thinking in terms of probabilities comes into play. While you cannot get every single bet right, as long as you get enough right and make enough money on those to offset your losses, you will make money in the long run.

It's not about getting one or two right. It's about executing the strategy with the best odds of winning over and over again and ensuring that your math works out with regards to the relationship between your win rate and average win.

So, it really comes down to finding patterns which repeat themselves over time in the markets. What causes these patterns? Well, the other traders of course! To put it more accurately, the orders that the other traders place in the market are what creates patterns that repeat themselves over time.

The first step to understanding these patterns is to understand what trends and ranges are. Identifying them and learning to spot when they transition into one another will give you a massive leg up not only with your options trading but also with directional trading.

Trends

In theory spotting a trend is simple enough. Look left to right and if the price is headed up or down, it's a trend. Well, sometimes it is really that simple. However, for the majority of the time you have both with and counter-trend forces operating in the market. It is possible to have long counter trend reactions within a larger trend and sometimes, depending on the time frame you're in, these counter-trend reactions take up the majority of your screen space.

Trend vs Range

This is a chart of the UK100 CFD, which mimics the FTSE 100, on the four-hour time frame. Three-quarters of the chart is a downtrend and the last quarter is a wild uptrend. Using the looking left to right guideline, we'd conclude that this instrument is in a range. Is that really true though?

Just looking at that chart, you can clearly see that short-term momentum is bullish. So, if you were considering taking a trade on this, would you implement a range strategy or a trending one? This is exactly the sort of thing that catches traders up.

The key to deciphering trends is to watch for two things: counter trend participation quality and turning points. Let's tackle counter trend participation first.

Counter Trend Participation

When a new trend begins, the market experiences extremely imbalanced order flow which is tilted towards one side. There's isn't much counter trend participation against this seeming tidal wave of with trend orders. Price marches on without any opposition and experiences only a few hiccups.

As time goes on though, the with trend forces run out of steam and have to take breaks to gather themselves. This is where counter trend traders start testing the trend and trying to see how far back into the trend they can go. While it is unrealistic to expect a full reversal at this point, the quality of the correction or pushback tells us a lot about the strength distribution between the with and counter-trend forces.

Eventually, the counter-trend players manage to push so far back against the trend that a stalemate results in the market. The with and counter-trend forces are equally balanced and thus the trend comes to an end. After all, you need an imbalance for the market to tip one way or another and a balanced order flow is only going to result in a sideways market.

While all this is going on behind the scenes, the price chart is what records the push and pull between these two forces. Using the price chart, we can not only anticipate when a trend is coming to an end but also how long it could potentially take before it does. This second factor, which helps us estimate the time it could take, is invaluable from an options perspective, especially if you're using a horizontal spread strategy.

In all cases, the greater the number of them, the greater the counter-trend participation in the market. The closer a trend is to ending, the greater the counter-trend participation. Thus, the minute you begin to see price move into a large, sideways move with an equal number of buyers and sellers in it, you can be sure that some form of redistribution is going on.

Mind you, the trend might continue or reverse. Either way, it doesn't matter. What matters is that you know the trend is weak and that now is probably not the time to be banking on trend strategies.

Starting from the left, we can see that there is close to no counter trend bars, bearish in this case, and the bulls make easy progress. Note the angle with which the bulls proceed upwards.

Then comes the first major correction and the counter-trend players push back against the last third of the bull move. Notice how strong the bearish bars are and note their character compared to the bullish bars.

The bulls recover and push the price higher at the original angle and without any bearish presence, which seems odd. This is soon explained as the bears slam price back down and for a while, it looks as if they've managed to form a V top reversal in the trend, which is an extremely rare occurrence.

The price action that follows is a more accurate reflection of the power in the market, with both bulls and bears sharing chunks of the order flow, with overall order flow in the bull's favor but only just. Price here is certainly in an uptrend but looking at the extent of the bearish pushbacks, perhaps we should be on our guard for a bearish reversal. After all order flow is looking pretty sideways at this point.

So how would we approach an options strategy with the chart in the state it is in at the extreme right? Well, for one, any strategy that requires an option beyond the near month is out of the question, given the probability of it turning. Secondly, looking at the order flow, it does seem to be following a channel, doesn't it?

While the channel isn't very clean, if you were aggressive enough, you could consider deploying a collar with the strike prices above and below this channel to take advantage of the price movement. You could also employ some moderately bullish strategies as price approaches the bottom of this channel and figuring out the extent of the bull move is easier thanks to you being able to reference the top of the channel.

As price moves in this channel, it's all well and good. Eventually though, we know that the trend has to flip. How do we know when this happens?

Turning Points

As bulls and bears struggle over who gets to control the order flow, price swings up and down. You will notice that every time price comes back into the 6427-6349 zone, the bulls seem to step in masse and repulse the bears.

This tells us that the bulls are willing to defend this level in large numbers and strongly at that. Given the number of times the bears have tested this level, we can safely assume that above this level, bullish strength is a bit weak. However, at this level, it is as if the bulls have retreated and are treating this as a sort of last resort, for the trend to be maintained. You can see where I'm going with this.

If this level were to be breached by the bears, it is a good bet that a large number of bulls will be taken out. In martial terms, the largest army of bulls has been marshaled at this level. If this force is defeated, it is unlikely that there's going to be too much resistance to the bears below this level.

This zone, in short, is a turning point. If price breaches this zone decisively, we can safely assume that the bears have moved in and control the majority if the order flow.

Turning Point Breached

The decisive turning point zone is marked by the two horizontal lines and the price touches this level twice more and is repulsed by the bulls. Notice how the last bounce before the level breaks produces an extremely weak bullish bounce and price simply caves through this. Notice the strength with which the bears break through.

The FTSE was in a longer uptrend on the weekly chart, so the bulls aren't completely done yet. However, as far as the daily timeframe is concerned, notice how price retests that same level but this time around, it acts as resistance instead of support.

For now, we can conclude that as long as the price remains below the turning point, we are bearishly biased. You can see this by looking at the angle with which bulls push back as well as, the lack of strong bearish participation on the push upwards.

This doesn't mean we go ahead and pencil in a bull move and start implementing strategies that take advantage of the upcoming bullish move. Remember, nothing is for certain in the markets. Don't change your bias or strategy until the turning point decisively breaks.

Some key things to note here are that a turning point is always a major S/R level. It is usually a swing point where a large number of with trend forces gather to support the trend. This will not always be the case, so don't make the mistake of hanging on to older turning points.

The current order flow and price action are what matters the most, so pay attention to that above all else. Also, note how the candles that test this level all have wicks on top of them.

This indicates that the bears are quite strong here and that any subsequent attack will be handled the same way until the level breaks. Do we know when the level will break? Well, we can't say with any accuracy. However, we can estimate the probability of it breaking.

The latest upswing has seen very little bearish pushback, comparatively speaking, and the push into the level is strong. Instinct would say that there's one more rejection left here. However, who knows? Until the level breaks, we stay bearish. When the level breaks, we switch to the bullish side.

Putting it all Together

So now we're ready to put all of this together into one coherent package. Your analysis should always begin with determining the current state of the market. Ranges are pretty straightforward to spot, and they occur either within big pullbacks in trends or at the end of trends.

Trends vary in strength depending on the amount of counter-trend participation they have. The way to determine counter trend participation levels is to simply look at the price bars and compare the counter-trend ones to the with trend ones. The angle with which the trend progresses is a great gauge as well, for its strength, with steeper angles being stronger.

Next, you need to determine the turning point of the trend. The turning point is a level that is extremely well defended by the with trend players and will be attacked repeatedly by the counter-trend traders in long trends.

Chapter 12 Sector Analysis: Technical and Fundamental

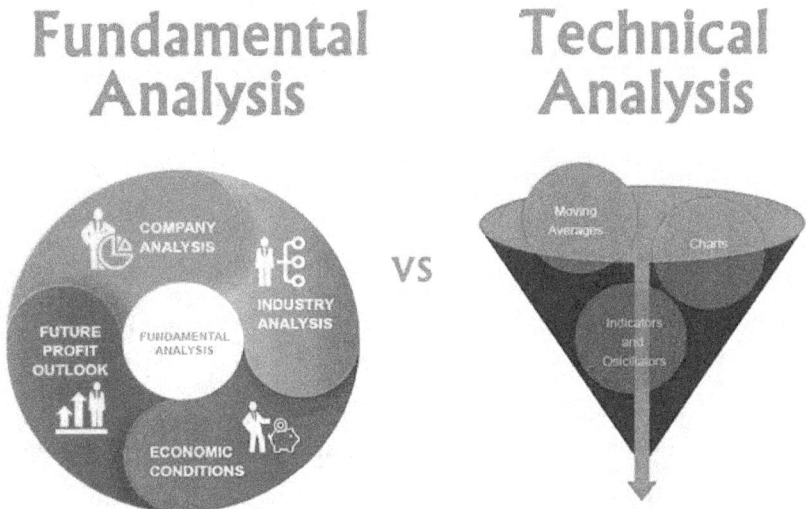

When working with technical analysis you are always going to want to remember that it functions because of the belief that the way the price of a given trade has moved in the past is going to be an equally reliable metric for determining what it is likely to do again in the future. Regardless of which market you choose to focus on, you'll find that there is always more technical data available than you will ever be able to realistically parse without quite a significant amount of help. Luckily, you won't be sifting through the data all on your own, and you will have numerous technical tools including things such as charts, trends, and indicators to help you push your success rates to new heights.

Understand core assumptions: Technical analysis is all about measuring the relative value of a particular trade or underlying asset by using available tools to find otherwise invisible patterns that, ideally, few other people have currently noticed. When it comes to using technical analysis properly you are going to always need to assume three things are true. First and foremost, the market ultimately discounts everything; second, trends will always be an adequate predictor of price and third, history is bound to repeat itself when given enough time to do so.

Technical analysis believes that the current price of the underlying asset in question is the only metric that matters when it comes to looking into the current state of things outside of the market, specifically because everything else is already automatically factored in when the current price is set as it is. As such, to accurately use this type of analysis all you need to know is the current price of the potential trade in question as well as the greater economic climate as a whole.

When it comes to technical analysis, the what, is always going to be more important than the why. That is, the fact that the price moved in a specific way is far more important to a technical analyst then why it made that particular movement. Supply and demand should always be consulted, but beyond that, there are likely too many variables to make it worthwhile to consider all of them as opposed to their results.

Chart Patterns to Be Aware Of

Flags and Pennants: Both flags and pennants show retracement, that is deviations that will be visible in the short term in relation to the primary trend. Retracement results in no breakout occurring from either the resistance or support levels but this won't matter as the security will also not be following the dominant trend. The lack of breakout means this trend will be relatively short term. The resistance and support lines of the pennant occur within a larger trend and converge so precisely that they practically form a point. A flag is essentially the same except that the resistance and support lines from the flag will be essentially parallel instead.

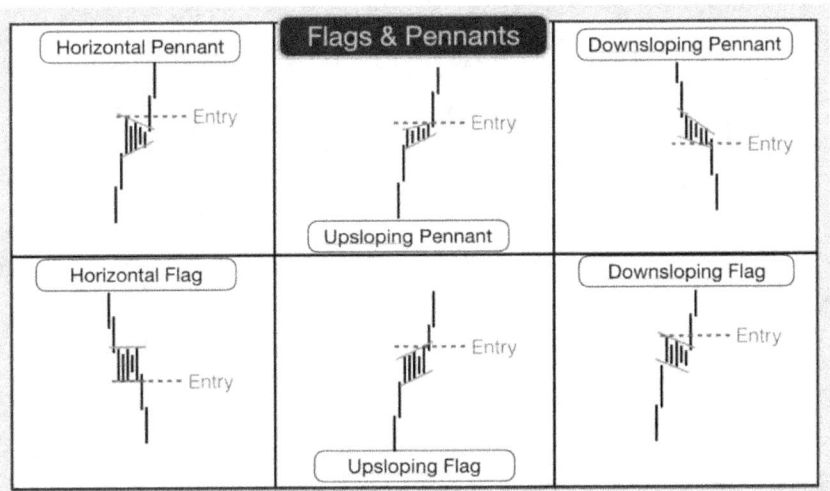

If you are looking for them, both flags and pennants are more likely to be found in the mid-section of the primary phase of the trend. They can last up to two weeks before being absorbed back into the primary trend line. They are typically associated with falling volume which means that if you notice a flag or a pennant and the volume is not falling then you are more likely actually seeing a reversal which is an actually changing trend instead of a simple retracement.

Head Above Shoulders Formation: If you are looking for indicators of how long any one particular trend is likely to continue, then looking for a grouping of three peaks in a price chart, known as the head above shoulders formation, can indicate a bearish pattern moving forward. The peaks to the left and to the right of the primary peak, also known as the shoulders, should be somewhat smaller than the head peak and also connect at a specific price. This price is known as the neckline and when it reaches the right shoulder the price will likely then plunge noticeably.

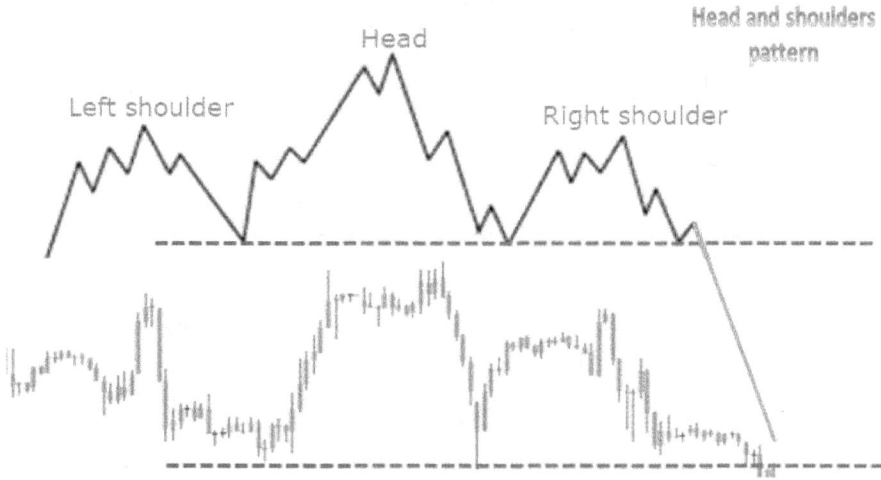

The inverse head and shoulders (or head and shoulders bottom) is a sign that the price of the security in question is about to rise in the face of an existing downward trend. It typically forms at the lowest overall price of the trend.

Based on the analysis of the peak-and-trough pattern from the Dow Theory, an upward trend is then seen as indicative of a series of successive rising troughs and peaks. Meanwhile, a downward trend is indicative of a series of lower peaks and deeper troughs. If this is the case, then the head and shoulders pattern represent a weakening of an existing trend as the troughs and peaks deteriorate.

The head and shoulders top forms at the peaks of an upwards trend and signals that a reversal is often forthcoming through a process of four steps. The first of these starts with the creation of the far-left shoulder which can be formed when the cryptocurrency reaches a new high before dropping to a new low. This is then followed by the formation of the head which occurs when the security reaches an even higher high before retracing back to the low found in the left shoulder. Finally, the right shoulder is formed from a high that is lower than the high found in the head, countered by a retracement back to the low of the left shoulder. The pattern is then completed when the price drops back below the neckline.

In both instances, the price dipping below the neckline signals the true reversal of the trend in question which means the security will now be moving in the opposite direction. This breakout point is often the ideal point to go either short or long depending. It is important to keep in mind, however, that the security is unlikely to continue smoothly in the direction the pattern suggests. As such, you will want to keep an eye out for what is called a throwback move.

Due to the fact that all times exist on the same line, the Gann angle can then also be used to predict resistance, support and direction strength as well as the timing on bottoms and tops as well. Gann angles are typically used to determine likely points of support and resistance and it is easy to get started with as it only requires the trade to determine the proper scale for the chart before drawing in the relevant Gann angles from the primary bottoms to the tops.

Essentially, this means that they make it less complicated for the trader to properly frame the market and thus makes it easier for them to predict the way the market is likely to move in the future based on the way it is currently moving in the predetermined framework. Angles that indicate a positive trend determine support and angles that show a downward trend outline resistance. This means that by understanding the accurate angle of a chart, the trader can more easily determine the best time to buy or sell far more simply than what could otherwise be the case. When utilizing Gann angles, it is crucial that you keep in mind all the different things that can potentially cause the market to change between specific angles.

Cup and handle formation: The cup and handle formation most commonly appear if given security reaches a peak price before dropping off significantly for a prolonged amount of time. Sooner than later, however, the security will rebound, which is the perfect time to buy. This is an indicator of a trend that is rapidly rising which means you are going to want to take advantage of it as soon as possible before you miss out.

The handle will form on the cup when those who purchased the security at the previous high-water mark and couldn't wait any longer begin to sell which makes new investors interested who then begin to buy as well. This type of formation does not typically form quickly, and indeed, has been known to take a year or more to become visible.

Ideally, you will then be able to take advantage of this trend as soon as the handle starts to form. If you see the cup and handle forming, you will still want to consider any other day to day patterns that may be interfering with the overall trend as they are going to go a long way when it comes to determining the actual effectiveness of buying in at a specific point.

Trend lines

Trend lines represent the typical direction that a given underlying asset is likely to move in and, thus, can be very beneficial for traders to highlight prior to trading. This is easier said than done, however, due to the high degree of volatility that assets of all types experience on a regular basis. As such, you will find it much more useful to consider only the highs and lows that the underlying asset experiences as this will make it far easier to determine a workable pattern. Once you have determined the highs and the lows for the underlying asset it then becomes much easier to determine if the highs are increasing while the lows are decreasing or vice versa. You will also want to remain alert to the possibility of sidewise trends, where the price doesn't move much of anywhere, as this is a sign that you should avoid trading for the time being. When watching the trend lines, you will likely notice that the price movement of a given underlying asset tends to bounce off the same high and low points time after time. These are what are known as resistance and support levels and identifying them makes it easier for you to determine the supply and demand of the coin in question. The support level is the level that the price is unlikely to drop below because there are always going to be traders who are willing to buy at that point, driving demand back up. Once the price reaches the point where traders feel the price is unlikely to go any higher, they start to sell, and a level of resistance is created.

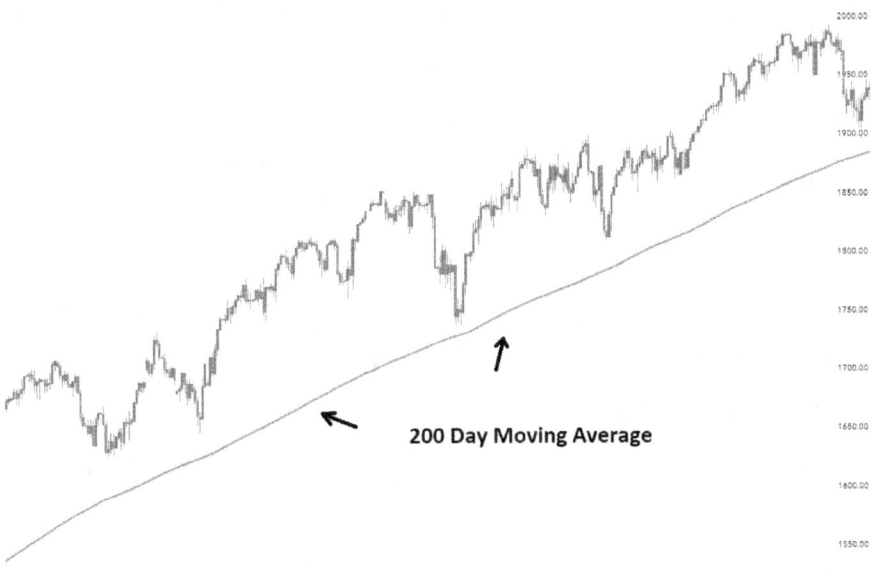

Moving averages: The most commonly used confirmation tool is one that is referred to as the moving average convergence divergence or MACD for short. This tool measures the amount of difference that there is between two averages that have been smoothed to minimize ancillary noise.

The difference between the two results is then further smoothed by the process before then being matched against the moving average that it relates to as well. If the resulting smoothed average is still greater than the existing moving average, then you can be sure that the positive trend you were chasing actually exists. Meanwhile, if the smoothed average ends up below the existing moving average than any negative trends will be confirmed instead.

The MACD chart is typically based on a combination of several EMAs. These averages can be based on any timeframe, though the most common is the 12-26-9 chart. This chart is typically broken into multiple parts, the first of which is the 26-day and 12-day chart. Mixing up the EMAs will allow you to more accurately gauge the level of momentum that the trend you are tracking is experiencing.

If the 12-day EMA ends up above the 26-day EMA, then you can assume the underlying stock in on an uptrend and the reverse indicates a downtrend. If the 12-day EMA increases more quickly than the 26-day EMA then the uptrend is going to be even more well-pronounced. However, if the 12-day EMA moves closer to the 26-day EMA then you can safely assume that it is starting to slow, and the momentum is waning, which means it is going to take the trend with it.

Chapter 13 Rolling Out Options

When it comes to making money trading options, it is important to remember that you must control your emotions at all times, something that is easier said than done, especially if you are in the moment and have just taken an unexpected loss. Cultivating the proper mindset can be done with practice, however, and doing so will make it easier for you to face the early parts of your options trading career with the proper expectations in regards to what sort of results you can expect from options trading. Specifically, this means that you will need to understand that investing in options isn't a quick and easy path to success and, rather, is sure to take plenty of dedication and hard work if you hope to see reap the potential rewards.

The first step to finding success via options trading is to get your emotions in check. The best traders are robotic, they only rely on the facts and they follow their trading plan 100 percent of the time. If you find yourself getting extremely emotional as far as trading is concerned then it is important that you start off by keeping a log of the emotions you have while trading, and the results of those emotions on your trading outcome. While this might seem unnecessary at first, you will be surprised how helpful having a clear outline of your personal patterns is when it comes to improving your overall trade percentage in the long term.

The fact of the matter is that if you ever hope to successfully trade options then you are going to need to know you can stick with your plan no matter what the emotional part of your mind is telling you to do. A good plan is one that remains successful, not 100 percent of the time, or even 95 percent of the time and instead manages to be successful roughly 60 percent of the time. While 60 percent is certainly enough to ensure you turn a profit, it is not enough that it allows for additional wiggle room in the terms of letting your emotions talking you into going off book at every turn. Remember, trading options is a numbers game and keeping your emotions in check is key to not working with skewed data.

Setting up a reasonable expectation

A trader who is staring up should always have the patience to wait to know a market and should not expect that he or she would large and handsome profit from their trading options. A new trader should never high expectation when they are just into the market. Rather they should be mentally prepared for losing capital rather than gaining capital. A trader should always begin to expect at least at a minimum market experience of a year or half. This can be illustrated very simply in any field. A famous successful person always bears time and patience to be the greatest achiever in their field.

Proof concept

If a trader starts off with the small trade, he or she will not only gain experience but will also save time. Noises of the stock market do not affect the small traders but if a trader starts with big trading options, he or she will react to these noises in the stock market. A new trader will be in a bad situation with such reactions and at the early time period. Starting with a small trade will teach a trader to manage capital which is very much necessary. A trader remembers all trades are not same in nature. A good trader will generate great ideas after the proper experience. A trader must always have records and check on them to see what idea works for them and what does not.

Proper sorting and record keeping

A good successful trader should always keep a record of few important things of the market like:

- The trader should keep a record of orders placed and quantity involved in it and money making out of it.

- The trader should keep in mind implied volatility and its reference to current condition.

- The trader should keep in mind about his competitors in the market in that particular trade.

- When the traders begin to keep a record and maintain records they begin to move towards success and chances of being in odd position is also reduced.

Good position of the trader

Once a trader has achieved his or her position in a trade or stock market, there are frequent ups and downs. A good position trader must know how to react to these situations. By small trade, he or she won't be much affected by the noise of the stock market.

The trader should keep in mind about buying stock exchange at the perfect time. When a trader does so, he or she can perfectly be in the market and understand well.

Proper evaluation of the position

A trader must decide very well that that few decisions like backing out on losses must be decided well according to perfect time.

There are few other decisions like a plan suddenly executed and whether he or she should move on with the profit or go for more?

Even if the sudden plan does not work out then he or she must have a backup and move on forward ahead and not repent on his or her loss and look for a new fresh start.

Hard work is the only way to success

It's easy to advise and listen to it. But when it comes up to the execution of the advice it's not that easy as things do not turn up the way it told.

The simple way is to start with small trade and have a lot of patience. A trader should make proper planning for execution. The trader should learn about the market and get into a good position and stick well to it and work very hard to achieve success and be a good disciplined successful trader.

At this point, it is time to move on to the next step. You already know some of the basics that come with working on options as well as some of their benefits.

Chapter 14 Designing A Trading Plan

Who starts off something without a plan? You need to have a plan for everything. Swing trading requires a plan too. A trading plan guides you in all your activities. A trading plan provides a routine for you and helps you become disciplined when you are trading. Far too many beginners set themselves up for trouble when they begin trading options by not having a plan. If you want to earn consistent profits when trading options, it is important to have a solid trading plan, and to be disciplined when carrying out your trades. These days, trading options is pretty easy. In some ways, that is a great thing. However, it can also lead people into trouble. If you just trade options on a whim, that can end up leading to quick losses.

Options prices can move fast. A simple moment of thought illustrates what can happen. Since the price of an option could move by $50, $75, or even $90 for a mere $1 rise or decline in the price of a share of stock, it's very easy for options prices to move very quickly. These rapid and dramatic price movements can create a lot of problems for new traders, and if you are only buying and selling individual call and put options, you are going to be very susceptible to these issues. If you were to buy five call options, and the stock price dropped by $1 with a delta of 0.75 over the course of ten minutes, you would lose $375.

And if you get in a situation like that, without a trading plan you won't be sure what to do. Often, stock prices can quickly reverse, and a $1 rise or fall of a stock price isn't all that significant for many of the most popular stocks, that have share prices that range from $100 to $2,000 per share. So, a $1 move in share price is not something necessarily unprecedented.

So, one of the problems with a big drop in price is that panic may ensue, and a novice trader will sell out to cut their losses. This can turn out to be a bad decision in many cases, and so selling options when there is a loss like that is not necessarily something that is the right decision. We will introduce the topic of technical analysis to help you learn ways to determine when to get in and out of trades, but the point here is that you need to have a plan in place rather than trading on emotional impulse.

This can work the other way as well. If the price of a share rises by $1, you could end up with significant gains (for the sake of example and simplicity, we are assuming that you are trading call options). One of the problems that happens with novice traders, is they get overwhelmed with irrational exuberance when share prices are rising. If the share price rises by $1, and you have five call options that rise in value by $345, it's easy to start having visions of making $1,000 in an afternoon. But of course, what often happens is a $1 rise in share price can suddenly turn into a $2 loss, and it can do that in a matter of minutes.

Trading Psychology

To avoid making these kinds of mistakes, it is important to adopt a trading psychology. In short, this means having a strict plan that you follow at all times. In a sense, you need to be detached from your trading on an emotional level, as if you were not the one risking the money. Of course, this is not something that is always easy to do. If you are losing your own hard-earned money, it can be difficult to detach yourself emotionally from what's going on.

The way to do this is to setup rules ahead of time and follow them. As a part of your trading psychology, becoming organized and disciplined is going to be something that you need to master. If you are not the kind of person who is organized and prone to detailed planning, then you will need to adjust your approach to things.

An important part of the trading psychology is not giving into emotion. As we mentioned in the introduction, you can fly into a panic when you get large losses, and you can also become excessively elated when you get gains. When you let emotion guide your trading decisions, you are going to find that you make a lot of mistakes. Sometimes, luck will be involved and so traders who are prone to making emotional decisions and not carefully planning out their trades are still going to have some impressive wins. This helps to keep them addicted and bring them back to make many trades, and if they get a big winning trade it will encourage them to keep following the same impulsive process hoping to hit another big win.

The best trading psychology is one that begins with a long-term plan. You should sit down and figure out what your long-term goals are over different time frames. First off, you need to be thinking in terms of reasonable gains. You are not likely to build success by hoping to make a million dollars right away. Instead, think in terms of making $100 a week, or $200 a week. Then map out a strategy that is going to help you actually realize your goals. Then once you have reached the goal, you can set a new goal to increase your income.

Trading options is not something that you can do if you have a "set it and forget it" attitude. As an options trader, although you don't necessarily have to be glued to your computer all day long, you need to be carefully tracking the movements in the share price of any underlying stock for your options. You don't want to impulsively buy an option (or ten options) and then go off and forget about them. You should be checking regularly to see how your options are doing, and possibly using electronic tools to setup alerts and so forth.

Value Education

The fact that you're reading this book is a great sign! Those who are willing to study and learn are definitely going to be more successful than those who simply start trading on impulse. But don't let this book be the end of your education, it should only be the beginning. There are many resources available for those who want to trade options, and you should continually take advantage of them. The more that you can learn about options trading, the more likely it is that you are going to be successful. You should watch as many videos as you can find, learn all the different ways and strategies that can be used when trading options, and read as many books and educational materials as possible.

You should look for official information about options that can help you learn the ropes from experienced traders. Many organizations that are associated with options trading have educational materials available. I also strongly recommend that you follow tasty trade. This is a group associated with the options trading platform Tasty Works, but you don't have to have an account with Tasty Works to use the educational platform. They have a large number of educational videos which are free to view on their website and on YouTube. They also have talk shows where they discuss different trading results, approaches to trading, and interviews with people who became successful options traders. Since it's free and put together by people who have been professional options traders for many decades in some cases, this is one of the best resources that you can use to educate yourself about trading options.

Use Buying and Selling Calls as a Learning Opportunity

Many novice traders have visions of making millions of dollars buying and selling individual call options. It is possible to make money trading individual call and put options, however very few professional traders make a career doing so. The fact is that straight trading of individual options is not likely to bring consistent and long-term success. It is just too difficult to consistently predict which way a stock price is going to move over short time periods.

That said, everyone has to start as a level 2 trader, and you can look at the period of time that you spend trading call and put options as a chance to gain some experience. At first, start with single options contracts until you get used to the mentality and experience of options trading.

As you train yourself, although many will be tempted to stick with call options because they are the way people think (you make money when the stock rises in price), you should also look for opportunities to make money from put options, and trade them. This will help your skills as an options trader broaden and improve, and you will start learning how to recognize trends in the markets that move in both directions.

Adopt a Trading Type

We haven't gotten into all the trading strategies yet. But by the time you finish reading this, you will understand all the main ways that you can trade options and the main strategies that are used by professional options traders. As you are learning, you can try your hand at all of them and find out which ones you enjoy the most and which ones you are best at trading.

However, you should winnow out your trading methods. The best professional traders are those that focus on using only one or two trading strategies. Options traders that become sellers of options premium typically only sell options premium. Of course, some people are able to multi-task more than others, and so they may have a more diversified strategy. The traders on Tasty Trade are often using many different strategies. That said, when you are new options trader, it is good to find one or two strategies and then master them. If you are able to work up a solid profit over the course of a year, then at that time you might want to expand your trading repertoire.

As another example, many traders like using iron condors to generate income. A large number of traders only trade iron condors. They have become expert at using this one technique, and so they spend their time looking for opportunities to apply the strategy and earning regular income.

Equipment and Location

Most options traders don't need a large amount of equipment. If you start saying the word "trader", you are probably approaching this issue thinking of day traders with banks of computer screens displaying lots of charts and tables. This is not necessary for the vast majority of options traders. You certainly should have a good desktop computer that you have access to, and optionally you should also have a smart phone or tablet you have access to as well. If you are using a trading platform that does not have a lot of analysis tools and you have to use a second website for that purpose, you might want to have a second desktop computer or use a second device like an iPad to be following stock charts and so forth. Most traders can get by with a good desktop computer, iPad, and smart phone. And of course, you will need a good internet and Wi-Fi connection. The last thing you want to do is get in a situation where you are needing to get out of a trade and your internet connection goes down. This is one reason why having a smart phone so that you can still access the trading platform when your internet is down is a good idea, rather than relying exclusively on a desktop computer.

Chapter 15 Advanced Strategies

The Call Back spread

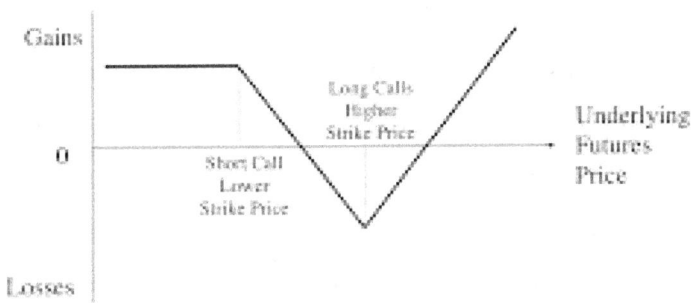

The back spread is an options strategy that traders take up when they perceive that the market will be very volatile, though not 100% sure on the direction of the price. The stock's significant movement in the preferred direction earns them a big profit, but if it only moves a little, the trader earns a little profit. If the stock fails to move at all, the trader suffers a loss. Back spreads are also called reverse ratio spreads because they are designed to behave in the opposite direction of the ratio spreads.

When you are bullish on a particular stock, the back-spread position you take is called the call ratio back spread, or simply, the call back spread. You enter this position when you buy a particular number of out-of-the-money call options (the kind whose strike price is more than stock value), and selling a smaller number of in-the-money call options (current stock price higher than the strike price). You have the liberty to choose the number of call options to sell or buy, but for now, let's only work with the case of a trader who buys 2 on-the-money call options then sells 1 in-the-money call option.

From buying the 2 call options and selling the 1 in-the-money call option, the trader has entered into what is called a credit position. This position allows the trader to earn a premium just by opening a call back spread. It happens when the trader buys the two call options, but since he is not willing to wait for the option to expire, he sells one option. However, even after the sale, the option owner still needs to buy back the option before it expires. These exchanges are what make taking this position quite risky.

If the stock price falls below the call option's strike price sold by the trader, then trader can allow the option to expire because, at this time, both strike prices are now meaningless. When this happens, the profit collected is the initial premium the trader made when he opened the position.

If the price of the stock rises high above the price of the strike price (in-the-money), but it is still below the strike price of the 2 calls, that the trader bought at the on-the-money price, the situation is no longer good.

The 2 calls purchased on-the-money would become worthless, but the call the trader sold at the in-the-money strike price would still be worth something. It will need to be bought back before the contract expires.

Once the stock price has risen above the in-the-money strike price, the profits you can receive are limitless. The value of the in-the-money call rises, and even then, it must be bought back. The cost of purchasing the option, however, will be negated by the trader's possession of the 2 calls he bought at the in-the-money strike price. What's more, the two calls' value will be rising quickly, and the trader can sell them at a profit.

As a put, the back spread functions the same way, only in the opposite direction, in a bearish position.

The Synthetic Short Stock

The synthetic short stock is an options trading strategy that takes the form of buying or selling a stock, but with call or put options. It is taken up when the trader is bearish on a particular stock, and it involves buying a put option, then selling a call option with the same expiry date and at the same strike price.

In a typical situation where a trader only buys the basic put option, no profits would be realized until the stock price begins to fall under the strike price a bit. On the other hand, if the investor decides to invest in put options, he will have to pay the full premium, with the maximum possible loss being that premium.

In the case of the synthetic short stock, however, a trader can begin to enjoy some profits, once the stock price falls under the strike price, and the amount made after selling the corresponding call option makes up for the premium the trader spends buying the put option.

The advantages of the synthetic short stock strategy come with a big pay-off, unfortunately. The trader is now exposed to unlimited losses. For example, the more and more the value of the stock increases, the more the money the investor needs to buy back his call option before it expires. This makes taking this position very expensive, especially if the trader had made a faulty prediction concerning the likely direction of the stock.

The opposite of the synthetic short stock is the synthetic long stock. It behaves in a directly opposite behavior and is used by traders who feel bullish about their position to a stock.

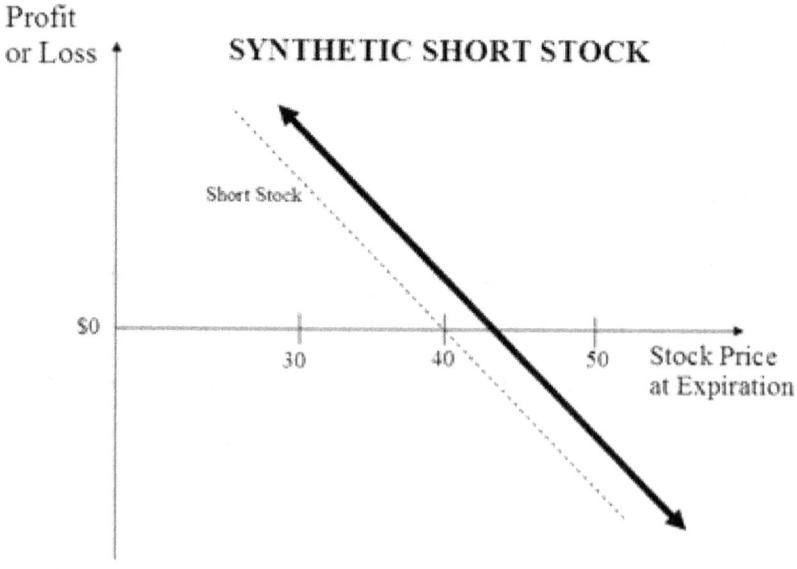

The Long Butterfly Spread

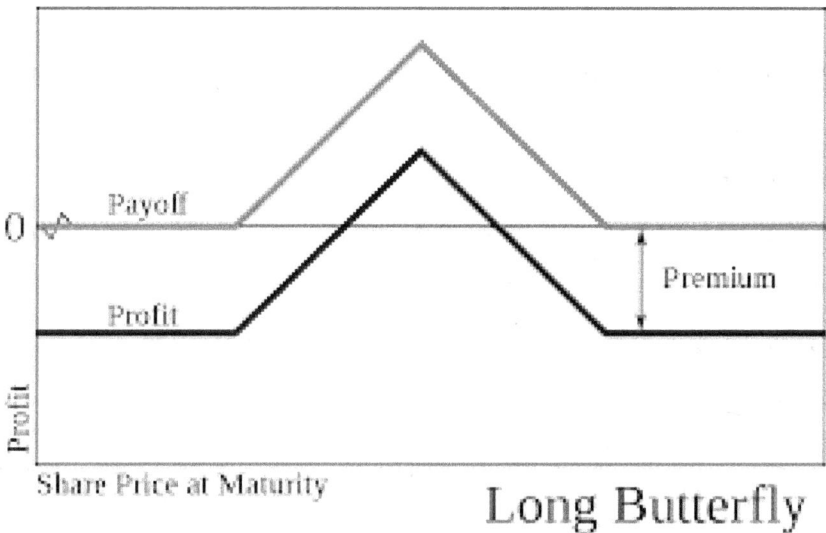

The Butterfly spread strategy is composed of 2 vertical spreads with a common strike price. The two spreads are the opening position where options are bought or sold, at 3 individual strike prices. These calls can be either calls or puts. The arrangement of the options makes the Butterfly spread a strategy that limits both profits and losses.

There is no difference between a Long Butterfly spread created with either calls or puts because, due to put-call parity, a Long Butterfly spread created out of put options behaves precisely like one created out of call options. Therefore, whichever you use, calls, or puts, you can create a Long Butterfly.

Take the example of a trader who purchases 1 in-the-money call option but sells 2 at-the-money call options, before purchasing another out-of-the-money call option. As you see, this strategy combines two opposing vertical spread options, which is how it got its name, the Butterfly Spread.

If you combine the profit profiles of the four call options mentioned above, you will realize that was the strike price to fall, the trader will only suffer limited losses. He would only lose the premium he paid trying to set up the entire butterfly arrangement. If the stock price were to climb very high, the losses would be limited too. However, if the stock price remained around the at-the-money strike price, the trader would receive some profit, but it too would be limited.

The Long Butterfly is thus a comfortably neutral strategy for when the market is experiencing low volatility because the trader will be making a correct bet, saying that the stock price would not be making much movement. Then he would receive the maximum profits, the limited ones we mentioned above.

Another advantage of the Butterfly strategy is that it is a low-risk approach. In case the stock climbs unexpectedly or crashes, the losses suffered will be limited.

The Short Butterfly strategy is just like the Long Butterfly strategy, but the roles are reversed. Its spreads are reversed, and it is taken up when the market is experiencing volatile shocks.

One keynote you ought to make regarding the Butterfly positions is that they involve three different strike prices, whether buying or selling options. To take it up, most brokers will ask you to pay 3 commissions to open the position, and you must pay 3 more commissions as you exit.

Therefore, keep these commissions in mind when weighing the possibility of taking the Butterfly. See whether it will be a profitable strategy, given your circumstances. (Of course, the fees paid will vary from one broker to the next).

The Long Iron Condor

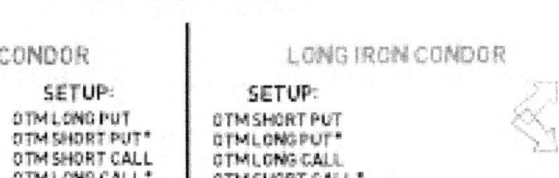

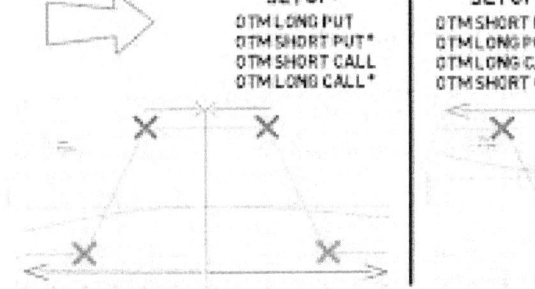

The Iron Condor strategies are an advanced strategy that, just like the Butterfly, uses two vertical spreads. The trader opens a call spread at a strike price higher than the current stock value of the underlying asset and opens a put spread too, at a strike price that is lower than the current stock value. Of the Iron Condor strategies, the Long Iron Condor is the most popular, and it is also one of the most preferred advanced options buying strategies.

Options trading instructors highly recommend it.

Using the Long Iron Condor strategy is similar to making a 'sure bet' although it leaves room for some modest profit and a few errors. The strategy is designed to be used on stocks that are not volatile, and those that maintain a neutral trading range. In addition, in case the stock price moves too much, and the option reaches its expiration date, the losses resulting from this are very high, although limited.

The way to go about opening the Long Iron Condor position is by creating a bullish put spread and a bearish call spread. You create the call spread by selling 1 out-of-the-money call option and purchasing another call option whose out-of-the-money position is further along. You create the put by selling 1 out-of-the-money put option and then purchasing 1 put option that is further out-of-the-money. The spreads you will have created are credit spread, and once the position is opened, you can expect to reap some income from them.

Having this unique spread together creates a target price range that falls between the inner out-of-the-money put strike price and the inner out-of-the-money call strike price. In the event the underlying stock price stays around this range by the time the expiry date comes, all four options will become worthless, and you get to keep the credit income you had at the start. If, however, the performance of the underlying stock becomes more volatile than you hoped and even gets out of the price range, you must close your in-the-money positions immediately. Unfortunately, doing this will reduce your profits and in the end, bring you a net loss.

In comparison to other neutral trading strategies, the Long Iron Condor stands out. If you compared it to similar strategies that deal with non-volatile stocks like the Strong Strangle and the Long Butterfly, you would note the differences. For example, if the price changes drastically, a trader using the Strong Strangle will suffer unlimited loss while a trader using the Long Iron Condor will only experience some limited maximum losses.

One significant disadvantage of the Long Iron Condor strategy is that it is made up of four individual options, and this could translate to higher commission costs, depending on the policies of your broker, in comparison to other strategies. What's more, the maximum loss potential that a trader stands to incur is often more than the initial credit income the trader placed when opening this position. These two factors are substantial, and they make the Long Iron Condor appear less profitable than people presume it to be. Therefore, before you take it up, it would serve you well to sit down and analyze all factors involved, weigh out the situation effectively, and see whether the strategy is appropriate for your trading goals. Do not forget to include the commission costs in your analysis.

The Long Strangle

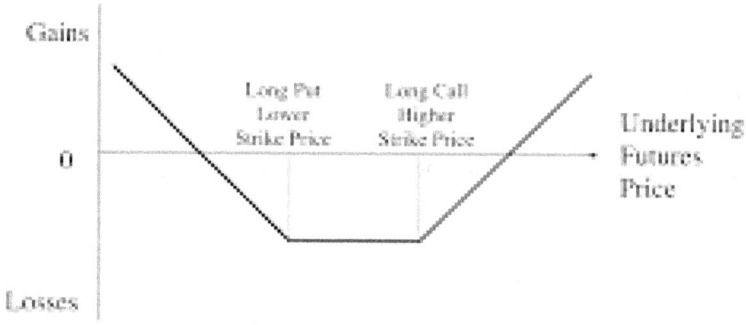

Strangle strategy options are strategies that thrive enable the trader's investments to thrive when the stock is volatile. The long strangle, for example, is the position a trader takes when anticipating high volatility in the underlying stock. The trader creates the Long Strangle position by purchasing 1 out-of-the-money call option, and 1 out-of-the-money put option. These options must share an expiration date.

Although the call option's stock price will be below the strike price, the call will not be worth anything, but once that stock price goes beyond the strike price, the call option will produce some profit. In the same way, the put option will be worthless so long as the stock price is above the option's strike price. However, once the strike price is higher than the stock price, the put option will begin to give some value.

When a trader brings together the two different profiles of the call and puts options, the result is the Long Strangle position. This strategy gives the trader the potential to make unlimited profits as the stock price climbs higher or falls lower.

Chapter 16 Key to A Successful Options Trading

The most recent decade saw dangerous development in the options trading market everywhere throughout the world.

Options are presently accessible on pretty much every comprehensible resource, from physical to financial resources. There currently is an ever-increasing number of classes of options available for trading on a single hidden resource alone.

The most recent decade additionally observed the touchy advancement of options trading training both on the web and disconnected. Understood financial gurus, for example, Robert Kiyosaki just as Masters 'O' Equity has been educating about the advantages of trading options around the globe, making mindfulness in what was prevalently a stock trading world.

In the present complex and vigorously traded options market, setbacks are made every day. Learners are losing money a lot snappier than they used to in stock trading and the subtle impeccable options strategy dependably appear to be so close yet so far away. All in all, the genuine inquiry options traders today are posing is, what precisely does it take to be useful in options trading?

Here are five keys to options trading achievement that I have closed after over a time of trading options.

1. Comprehend Your Trading Needs

A standout amongst the best things about options trading is that there isn't just a single method for trading. If you can control your feelings and have sufficient energy to trade amid the day, you could decide to day trade or force trade options. If you resemble the vast majority of us who might want to put on a trade and the sell it a couple of days or weeks after the fact at a superior cost, you may swing trade options. If you are scientifically disposed of and might want to put on a situation for fixed unsurprising income, you should need to contemplate increasingly about position trading.

Day trading, force trading, swing trading, and position trading are the four fundamental approaches to trade options. Choosing which approach to seek after is essentially a component of the measure of time you can submit and your tendencies.

2. Comprehend Your Chosen Strategy

There are likewise numerous approaches to benefit from day trading, swing trading, or position trading options. These techniques go from easy to involve. Regardless of what strategy you seek after, you have to comprehend the procedure completely, its advantages and disadvantages just as hazard profile. This incorporates its most significant benefit and misfortune just as the conditions under which they happen. Understanding an options strategy goes past only acing the counts yet, also, seeing how you may respond to all the potential results of the plan. Continuously paper trade for an extended period with the goal that you experience every one of its advantages and disadvantages before applying for actual money.

3. Pick the Right Stock

Each choice strategy benefit when the underlying stock performs with a particular goal in mind and loses money when the stock doesn't. Regardless of which strategy you choose to seek after, you should probably pick stocks that perform in that very manner. In that capacity, great principal and specialized examination aptitude are essential to options trading achievement. The specialized investigation is of specific significance in options trading since the precise passage and leaves focuses are critical for options, being a period touchy financial instrument.

4. Hazard Management

Regardless of what options strategy you choose to seek after, there is an opportunity of losing money. A few options procedures have restricted hazard while some have significant risk. Constrained risk implies that it can just drop a fixed measure of money regardless of how terrible things turn out. Every active alternative trader chooses how much risk to take for each trade in the system of their general portfolio chance administration approach. This will oversee the number of agreements to business (position estimating) and where to set their stop misfortune.

For example, when you have a ten thousand dollars account, wishes to seek after a straightforward long call options strategy and choose not to lose more than 10% per trade, you would submit close to one thousand for every business.

5. Benefit Taking Strategy

Acknowledging how to apply the correct alternatives strategies to the correct stocks with proper peril, the official's technique set up looks like acknowledging how to fly a plane. In spite of the fact that making sense of how to take off and investigate perceptible all around is huge, it is the ability to show up the airplane safely in the correct objective that makes a pro pilot. Acknowledging when and how to take advantage suitably takes after getting a flight. Such countless disciples lamentably hold a position directly from enthusiasm into a significant disaster. To fuel the circumstance, the obliged future of alternatives contracts doesn't empower incredible time for such difficulties to return up.

Risk Management Strategies

Following Market Trends:

Numerous investors accept that contributing against the market patterns can yield them higher returns. Notwithstanding, following the pattern is one of the most significant securities trade techniques to moderate investment opportunity. The trouble in this technique is having the option to distinguish the pattern on the grounds that the business sectors are dynamic and always showing signs of change. Having the option to detect the transient patterns inside the more extended term is a troublesome assignment.

Diversifying Investment Portfolio:

The Indian securities trade gives investors a few financial items, for example, values, securities, subsidiaries, and common assets. Investors can decide on more than one of these financial instruments to broaden their portfolios. Further enhancement can be accomplished by including financial items offered by various organizations, having a place with particular segments. This shields the general return from the investments from market variances and if a particular division or organization moves in an ominous manner, different interests in the portfolio can accomplish the equalization inside the investors' portfolios.

Being Patient and Avoiding Quick Decisions

A few financial specialists settle on speedy and rushed choices, and with each, little development in the cost of their investments. Besides, another financial trade tip that investors neglect to hold fast to, is setting aside the effort to do their exploration and due determination before settling on their offer market venture choices. Deciding the financial goals before contributing and concentrating on both present moments just as long-term results will enable financial specialists to appreciate greatest profits for their securities trade investments.

Planning the Trades:

Arranging and building up the system helps win wars. This is valid reason for putting resources into the Indian securities trade as well. Pre-arranging can have a significant effect among progress and disappointment through stock trading. Utilizing stop-misfortune and take-benefit focuses are valuable instruments in arranging the trades. Fruitful investors pre-decide the passage and leave value levels to figure the potential returns against the capability of the shares hitting these value levels. Then again, ineffective dealers make investments without considering the costs at which they will purchase and sell the financial instruments. They frequently trade with feelings; they keep clutching their positions; notwithstanding, when the value diminishes, in the expectation of a turnaround, and neglect to book profits when the value ascends with the eagerness of making higher profits.

- Stop-Loss:

This is the most reduced value that the financial specialist is happy to sell and avert further loss. Setting a stop-loss point is valuable when the market doesn't move according to the financial specialist desires. It is advantageous in averting the "cost will return" attitude and restricting the loss on the venture.

Take-Profit:

This is the cost at which the investor is eager to sell his venture and book profits. This point is useful to lessen the dangers when the probability of further cost increment is gigantic. Booking profits on stocks that are nearing their obstruction levels after huge increase, guarantees that investors sell these before solidification happens and costs start to diminish.

The financial trade is dangerous and shrewd investors exploit risk the executive's systems to relieve it. Cautious and auspicious utilization of different risk relief devices guarantees financial specialists can amplify profits through stock trading.

Chapter 17 Top Trader Mistakes to Avoid in Options Trading

Beginning your trading career by buying out-of-the money options. Many times, novice option traders buy calls because it seems to be a strategy similar to equity purchases. The strategy is the same, buy when the strike price is low, and sell when the underlying asset price has rallied. Unfortunately, picking a winner when buying out-of-the-money calls is very difficult. If you consistently use this strategy only, you will lose money and never know what you are doing wrong.

What is the hard part about buying calls?

You have to not only pick a stock winner, and predict the movement up or down, you also have to get the timing just right. While your underlying assets sits in the fridge molding, the time that the option expires is getting closer. If you buy a near-term out-of-the-money option, that time will expire faster than you desire.

Most novice traders pick these types of options because the price is low. Unfortunately, the options are cheap for a reason. Just because you bought it, and it increases over your purchase price, doesn't mean it will reach and extend beyond the strike price. The likelihood of the stock moving where you want it is very small.

The cost of the out-of-the-money option reflects this negative probability in the cheap price. If you insist on buying an out-of-the-money option, sell an OTM call in a covered call with an underlying asset you have in your holdings. When selling your call, you have agreed to sell your asset at the strike price placed in the option. Your statement is: if my stock increases to the strike price and beyond, I'll sell you the stock and you can "call" me on it. Your payday will be the strike price minus the original price of the underlying asset plus the call premium.

You have risk when you purchase the underlying asset, but not when you sell your option. Your maximum potential loss will be the cost of the underlying asset, minus the premium for the call. You will not lose an abundant capital amount, but you will lose the obvious potential for more profit if the stock greatly exceeds your strike price.

On the other hand, if the stock doesn't move, you get the premium for the call and get to keep the stock. If the stock tanks, you can exit by purchasing the option back, closing your short position, and then selling the underlying asset to end the long position. This may result in losing some shares of stock.

A better solution:

A low-risk option strategy is selling your covered calls. This will glean income and help your experience with options trading. While waiting for the option to close, you can see how the market fluctuates and the prices of the options that change in relationship to the surrounding volatility.

Using one options strategy for all situations

One of the best things about trading options is the flexibility of your choice of strategies. You can take advantage of this opportunity no matter what the market condition, as long as you are learning and testing new strategies. Do not limit yourself to one strategy when there are so many that are successful.

Buying a long spread is a great way to adapt to the changing market and reap a profit.

What if you leave the play too soon and miss some profit?

This is the nightmare that traders dream. Turn the equation this way:

What if I (the trader) learn to reduce my losses by better trades, evaluate my moves with more consistency and profit for the payoff, and stop having nightmares?

Using your trading plan will give you better results. Record the strategies and look back to see what worked for you and what did not. Practice using the strategies successfully to perfect your trading methods.

A better solution:

It doesn't matter if you are buying or selling, you must have a clear exit plan. Study the opportunity for profit and write down how much you want to gain if the stock rallies. Study the worst scenario and write down what you are willing to lose. If you get to the rally and your price, terminate the position and take your payday. Don't let greed interfere with logic.

If you hit the stop-loss from an underlying stock nose-dive, terminate your position and remove your exposure. Do not gamble that you will have a rebound. Take the loss and move on.

You will be tempted to throw this advice out the window so you can make one more trade to recover your loss. Don't give in to temptation. Make your trading plan and stay with the plan. Do you remember I said write it down? Writing it down will imprint it more firmly in your mind and will also serve as a reminder right in front of you to stick with the program.

Don't chase your emotions when you are placing trades.

Don't compromise your capital account by doubling up trades to recover losses.

Many people, including traders, use the word never capriciously. I will "never buy ITM options", for example. This is a silly way to think because you don't know what you'll do if you are desperate, and we are desperate when the trades are tanking.

Every trader has been in the losing circle. When you get there, everything hurts, especially your pride and your wallet. You may even think, if I just double up I can catch up the losses for the day. You won't. You will lose even more money because you are thinking with your emotions. Your judgement is impaired. You will make mistakes and you will enter trades that you would not have even considered when you had a clearer head.

Losses are not personal. The stock market does not have a vendetta against your trades. Sometimes the market wobbles and wiggles and the trades fall down. Do not EVER try to recoup your losses by making ill-advised trades.

A better solution:

Doubling up options is not the same as doubling up on stocks. Options are called derivatives because they are valued by their underlying asset. The prices, the movement, and the volatility is not the same as the stock. Your time decay has to be included into the plan for the trade.

When the trade is going south, ask "Would I have done this when I executed this position?" If the answer then was "no", the answer now should be the same.

Leave the trade, cut the loss, or look for a better opportunity with a different strategy. This trade obviously is not working so give it up. If it blows up, take the minor loss so you won't have a major loss later that will really hurt your pocketbook.

Do not trade illiquid options

Liquidity is how fast the trader can buy and sell an underlying asset without causing a major price move for the stock. Active buyers want a liquid market that is stable and moves, as do sellers.

Traders want a stable stock that can be converted into cash quickly, and at a good price. The blue-chip stocks are stable stocks and can bought and sold quickly. Often their sell price is only pennies in difference when they are exchanged. These are examples of stocks with good liquidity. The next sale of the stock will be within cents of the price of the last sell.

The selling of stocks on the stock exchange is much more liquid than trading options for one reason, stock trades are one stock, but options may be dozens of contracts. The stock trades are based on mostly common stock, but the options can be more than a half dozen. Just because there are more opportunities and selections mean the options will not be as liquid as stocks.

Illiquid stocks are stocks that trade once a week, or by appointment only. Their prices are very favorable, but their movement is not. This makes the gap between the bid and the asking price for the option to be unnaturally wider. As an example, our Blue Wide stock that cleans up the ocean has a bid-ask spread of $.25. The bid is $1.75, and the ask is $2.00, if you purchase the $2.00 contract you have paid 10% to establish the option. You have now purchased an option with a 10% loss before the trade has been executed. This does not bode well for this trade.

A better solution:

Illiquid options are a strangler for your money, they are more expensive in the long run, hard to unload, and usually a bust. Don't get involved in a stale stock, it will make you weep.

Open interest

Open interest is defined as the quantity of open contracts at a specific strike price and a specific date of expiry that are bought or sold on a given day to open the position. Opening contracts increases the open interest and closing contracts will decrease the calculation. The open interest integer is derived at the close of the bell each day.

If you are options trading, the open interest should be 40 times the contract quantity you are interested in trading. If you are trading 10-lots, the liquidity for you to make the trade will safely be 10 times 40, or 400 open contracts.

Look for liquid trade options so that you will not have more nightmares and stress. Don't gamble on a risky situation, you will just lose money, time, and maybe a few hairs from the top of your head.

Make sure you remember the dividend and earnings payment dates when you figure your option.

The underlying stock can be assigned early if there is a big dividend in the calendar. If you are selling calls, the dividend increases your chances of assignment. Option owners do not have the privilege of collecting dividends. To do that, you have to buy the underlying stock.

Early assignment is a threat for all options contracts, but dividends are one of the threats you can avoid decreasing your probability of being assigned.

When earnings season hits, options contracts become more expensive, regardless of whether they are puts or calls. Pending economic announcements will create volatility with the underlying asset price. Be aware that earnings season is a more expensive endeavor. It might be a better idea to wait and see the effect of the economic announcements on the stock value.

A better solution:

Don't sell options that are pending a dividend, unless you are okay with the increased risk of assignment. If you trade during earnings season know that you'll pay more for the option and will incur more volatility in the underlying asset. If you must buy an option during the premium earnings season, buy a spread (buy 1 option and sell 1 option). If your option buy is increased in price, so will your sell option be.

Use Index Options to your advantage

When earnings announcements are released a stock, can become very volatile. The stock can go through many ups and downs if the announcement is unexpected, like a company layoff or reorganization. In contrast, the company that is on the S&P 500 won't rock the index as vehemently.

If our trader picks options based on the S&P 500 index, for example, this is protection against the economic announcements that occur for individual assets.

Use neutral trades on the major indices to minimize the impact of economic announcements.

A better solution:

Trade option strategies like short spreads if the market is stagnant. Choose the indices to give protection against sudden announcements that can cause a stock to waffle. Indices are much less likely to be impacted by volatile news. The short spread is constructed like the long spread but works in the opposite way.

Conclusion

Thank you for making it through to the end of Options Trading, let's hope it was informative and able to provide you with all of the tools you need to achieve your goals whatever they may be.

You should have the discipline to do your very own research, screen your own positions and monitor every one of the points of interest you may leave to your full-benefit financial firm. You can never again depend on a broker to watch your positions and call with guidance or suggestions. You are currently an autonomous administrator — and, all things considered, must be absolutely in charge of your own behavior.

You should likewise be mindful and be prepared to react to both fast moves in everyday trading designs and consistently evolving longer-term economic situations.

The next step is to continue your education in options trading and open a brokerage account and start trading. Start trading in small amounts and work your way up, so that you are not taking reckless risks, but instead building up experience and a sustainable business that can help you reach a zone where you are able to live a life of financial independence. Be sure to read my other books on stock trading, so you can learn about your other possibilities when it comes to trading and investing in the stock market and beyond.